IN THE *TRUE BLUE*'S WAKE

THE AMERICAN SOUTH SERIES
Elizabeth R. Varon and Orville Vernon Burton, Editors

In the *True Blue's* Wake

*Slavery and Freedom among the
Families of Smithfield Plantation*

DANIEL B. THORP

UNIVERSITY OF VIRGINIA PRESS

Charlottesville and London

University of Virginia Press
© 2022 by the Rector and Visitors of the University of Virginia
All rights reserved
Printed in the United States of America on acid-free paper

First published 2022

9 8 7 6 5 4 3 2 1

Library of Congress Cataloging-in-Publication Data
Names: Thorp, Daniel B., author.
Title: In the *True Blue*'s wake : slavery and freedom among the families of
    Smithfield plantation / Daniel B. Thorp.
Other titles: American South series.
Description: Charlottesville : University of Virginia Press, 2022. | Series:
    The American South series | Includes bibliographical references and
    index.
Identifiers: LCCN 2021035022 | ISBN 9780813947235 (hardcover ; acid-
    free paper) | ISBN 9780813947242 (ebook)
Subjects: LCSH: Preston family. | Smithfield Plantation House (Blacksburg,
    Va.)—History. | Slaves—Virginia—Blacksburg—History—18th century.
    | Slaves—Virginia—Blacksburg—History—19th century. | African
    American families—Virginia—Blacksburg—History—18th century. |
    African American families—History—19th century. | African American
    families—History—20th century. | African American families—
    Genealogy.
Classification: LCC F234.B59 T47 2022 | DDC 975.5/785—dc23
LC record available at https://lccn.loc.gov/2021035022

Cover art: William McNorton. (Collection of the Sanders County Historical Society)

*To the memory of all of those who were enslaved at Smithfield,
but especially to those whose names and stories remain unknown*

❖ CONTENTS ❖

❖ ACKNOWLEDGMENTS ❖

I would like to express my deep appreciation for the welcome and support I have received over the years from so many descendants of the Fraction, McNorton, and Moon families. Kerri Moseley-Hobbs, Lisa Davis, Valarie McCullar, Carole Crowder-King, Donald King, Scott Graves, Saunders Moon, Ruth Hatcher, Brandon Duncan, Burmeta Wagstaff Marlin, Robin Wagstaff, Elliot Mason, Rochelle McNorton, Vanessa McNorton, Todd Porter, and Marie Hart have patiently answered my questions and welcomed me into their extended families. I also want to acknowledge the assistance of Erica Conner (Montgomery County Courthouse), Sherry Hagerman (Sanders County Historical Society), and Zoe Ann Stoltz (Montana Historical Society) in securing material from their collections and to thank Stewart Scales for making my map and Leslie King for helping to format the photographs. Jack Davis, Warren Milteer Jr., Colita Nichols Fairfax, and an anonymous reader each helped to make it a better book through their careful reading and thoughtful comments, and the Department of History, the College of Liberal Arts and Human Sciences, and the Faculty Publication Program at Virginia Tech each provided financial support for the publication of this book. I am grateful to them all.

Finally, I want to thank my wife, Elizabeth, for her constant and enthusiastic support of this project, even when it got us lost on the backroads of eastern Maryland.

❖ A NOTE ON LANGUAGE ❖

Race has long been a contentious subject in the United States. Recently, though, even the language we use to discuss race has become controversial and politicized. In such an environment it seems appropriate to me, as the author of the words contained in this book, to say a little about the thinking behind them. This is not intended to criticize any other writers or to argue that my choices were correct. It is simply to explain my decisions.

While I was writing this book, a number of publishers and writers were questioning why "black" and "white" were not capitalized when ethnic and national groups have long been treated that way. Because of the way they were brought to this country, most Black Americans have long been identified by the color of their skin rather than the specific ethnic or cultural community to which they belong. And in a change from historical precedent, White Americans seem to have become more likely to identify themselves as White than as Anglo-American or German American. Thus, it makes sense to many writers, and to the *Chicago Manual of Style*, to capitalize Black and White when those terms refer specifically to a racial and ethnic identity, either as nouns or adjectives. I have chosen to follow that pattern.

"Slave" is a different matter. There has been less public debate about this, but there have been discussions within the scholarly community about using or avoiding the word slave. Some writers and editors have expressed frustration with the repeated use of "enslaved individuals." Others, however, have stressed the dehumanizing effect of identifying a human being as a piece of property. Slavery was a brutal system that traumatized many of those who were trapped in it, and the memory of that trauma still affects the lives and thinking of many people descended from its victims.

In researching this book, I worked closely with descendants of several of the families who were enslaved at Smithfield and did not want to write about their families in a way that caused them any additional discomfort. My conversations with these descendants led me to understand that what they objected to was using the word slave to describe particular individuals and, in doing so, stripping them of their humanity and making their status as property the defining element of their identity. As a result of these conversations, I adopted the practice of using the word slave, or slavery, to describe the institution generally, and its victims collectively, but avoided the term when describing specific individuals.

I appreciate the insights of my editors, the reviewers of my manuscript, and the descendants of the families described in this book. Ultimately, however, the language used here is mine, and the choices made were mine. They are not a question of politics. They are a sign of respect.

IN THE *TRUE BLUE'S* WAKE

Introduction

T he *True Blue* was a slave ship that sailed out of Liverpool during the third quarter of the eighteenth century. It made at least nineteen trips across the Atlantic between 1756 and 1776 and carried several thousand enslaved men and women from West Africa to British colonies in the Caribbean or on the North American mainland. On one of those voyages in 1759, the *True Blue* took 280 captives from a coastal trading post in what is now Ghana to a tiny port in southern Maryland. There, a young man named William Preston purchased sixteen of the stolen souls on board and took them away to an unknown fate.[1]

Eighty-four years later, in May of 1843, James Patton Preston, one of William Preston's sons, died at Smithfield, a plantation his father had established in southwest Virginia shortly before the American Revolution. James Patton Preston had inherited and expanded Smithfield and was a very wealthy man when he died. Like many wealthy men of his day, he left an extensive estate that was carefully inventoried by his executors in order to settle his accounts and facilitate the division among his heirs of whatever property remained after Preston's debts were paid. Part of that inventory consisted of a list naming and assigning a price to each of the ninety-one men, women, and children enslaved at Smithfield when Preston died.

It is impossible to say with certainty that any of the ninety-one individuals named on that inventory were, in an actual biological sense, descended from any of the sixteen people that William Preston bought off the *True Blue* in 1759. Symbolically, though, all of them were. The men and women Preston bought in 1759 represented his first venture into the market of human beings as chattel, and as a result of that endeavor he decided that enslaved workers were a commodity in which he intended to continue investing. Thus, over the next twenty years, William Preston built a considerable fortune off the labor of enslaved workers, and his son, James Patton Preston, followed in his father's footsteps. Every one of the ninety-one people that James Patton Preston held in bondage in 1843 was at Smithfield because the purchase that Preston's father made in 1759 had worked so well to the family's advantage. In that sense, each of the ninety-one individuals named in 1843 was a direct descendant of those who arrived aboard the *True Blue*.

That 1843 inventory was also the genesis of this book. It is the most complete surviving picture of the enslaved community at Smithfield between the plantation's founding in 1774 and the collapse of slavery there in 1865. And while it is a snapshot of a single moment in time, it provided a starting point from which to undertake a broader exploration reaching back into the eighteenth century and forward to the twenty-first. The inventory and a variety of other records touching upon these ninety-one individuals, their ancestors, and their descendants made it possible to identify many of those included on the inventory as distinct individuals and to reconstruct many elements of their lives before and after the day on which their names and ages were recorded as property of the estate that held them in bondage.

Smithfield is often described as one of the first plantations west of the Blue Ridge Mountains, and it looms large in the history of southwest Virginia. Its founder, William Preston, played a major role in European settlement of the New River Valley and in integrating that region into Virginia and the United States during the tumultuous years of the American Revolution. In the decades that followed, Smithfield was the seat of an extended family that spread across the antebellum South and produced dozens of state legislators, three governors, ten members of Congress, two cabinet members, and a vice president of the United States. William Preston and his descendants were among the most influential settlers and developers of the southern Appalachian region, and historians of the region have long celebrated their activities and impact.

Historians have said much less, however, about the hundreds of Africans and African Americans whose labor made the Prestons' success possible. Indeed, historians of southwest Virginia have often written as if slavery did not exist at all in the region. Enslaved Africans, however, reached southwest Virginia almost as early as White settlers did, and by the early nineteenth century they were a significant element in the region's population and economy. Admittedly, their numbers were smaller than those found farther east, but in Montgomery County, where Smithfield stands, enslaved African Americans made up 13 percent of the county's population by 1810, and fifty years later that figure had climbed to 21 percent. Nor were these generally domestic workers living in White households with small numbers of other enslaved domestic workers. By the close of the antebellum era, a majority of those held in slavery in Montgomery County lived on holdings with ten or more enslaved workers, and a third lived on plantations with twenty or more.[2]

For families like the Prestons and plantations like Smithfield, the significance of slavery should be obvious: enslaved workers helped build a home the Prestons occupied for more than a century and that visitors continue to admire today. Those same workers cleared hundreds of acres of land surrounding that home, and their labor on that land and in that house made possible the Prestons' luxurious standard of living and underlay their significant social and political influence. Yet despite the obvious importance of slavery at Smithfield, the individual men, women, and children held in that institution have long remained unrecognized. Like the land or the climate, they have been taken for granted and rarely seen for their own sakes. Only recently have scholars begun trying to reconstruct the identities and experiences of those who made up the workforce at Smithfield and other Preston properties in southwestern Virginia. This book builds on that modest beginning in an effort to tell as fully as possible the stories of the men, women, and children enslaved at Smithfield. And while it began as an investigation of the ninety-one people named in the inventory of James Patton Preston, it is not restricted to that group. Both Smithfield and its population changed and grew between 1774 and 1865. William Preston established the original plantation and its workforce during the 1770s. After Preston's death, the land that was Smithfield passed intact to his widow and to his son James Patton Preston, but many of those who lived and worked there were distributed among Preston's other children as they came of age, and they were often moved to other locations. Then when James Patton Preston died, Smithfield's land was divided among his three sons and became three contiguous plantations—a smaller Smithfield, Solitude, and White Thorn—while the ninety-one enslaved individuals named on the inventory of Preston's estate were divided among those same three sons and his only surviving daughter. Meanwhile, those sons purchased additional workers on their own or acquired them through their wives when they married. Thus, the enslaved population of the family complex centered on Smithfield grew over time.

More than two hundred individuals were enslaved at the original Smithfield or on the plantations carved out of it between 1774 and the abolition of slavery there in 1865. This book seeks to tell their stories: who they were, what they experienced in slavery, and what they and their families accomplished after gaining their freedom. Those identified on the inventory of James Patton Preston provided a starting point for my research, but with them stand dozens of others enslaved before or after 1843. Details are often scarce in the biographies of enslaved people. In the case of Smithfield, it is impossible even to say with certainty how many people were enslaved there between 1774 and 1865, much less who they all were, what they all did, or where they all went following their emancipation. All of them, however, lived in the wake of the *True Blue,* and this is their story.

Slavery Comes to Smithfield

I n August of 1759 a British ship named the *True Blue* docked near the
mouth of Nanjemoy Creek, which flows into the Potomac River in
Charles County, Maryland. The *True Blue* was a slave ship based in
Liverpool, and it represented one small piece in the massive international
trade that over several centuries carried millions of men, women, and children from the lives they knew in Africa to hellish slavery in the Americas.
By the mid-eighteenth century, this trade was well-established. Ships like
the *True Blue* arrived regularly at large forts built along the African coast by
European companies or governments. There they traded a range of European goods, including guns and ammunition, for captive people brought
to the forts by African traders living nearby. Using the goods and weapons
acquired in these exchanges, the traders went back into the interior to purchase or capture additional victims and bring them to the coast. There they
were sold to the Europeans in exchange for more goods and more guns, and
the cycle continued.[1]

On this particular voyage, the *True Blue* had sailed from Liverpool to
Anomabu Castle, on the coast of what is now Ghana. Anomabu was one
of several British slave markets on the African coast during the eighteenth
century, and at any given time, hundreds of captives from across West
Africa waited in their cells and pens for the arrival of ships like the *True
Blue*. Those aboard the *True Blue* in 1759 were advertised as "Gold Coast
slaves" and probably represented a mix of peoples from the interior regions
of modern Ghana. They were almost certainly a mix of adults and children,
male and female. Adult men may have been the most desirable plantation

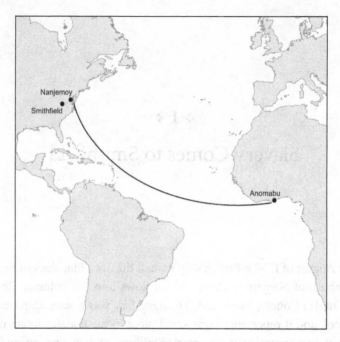

The voyage of the *True Blue*. (Map by Stewart Scales)

workers, but not everyone could afford a "prime hand," and merchants wanted to ensure they could accommodate a range of customers. Some of those carried on board the *True Blue* were probably soldiers captured in battle by armies of the expanding Ashanti Empire; others may have been sent into slavery to settle a debt or a judicial dispute; while others may have been farmers or artisans living peacefully in their villages until they were seized by armed raiders. Once enslaved they may have been sold several times in smaller, inland markets before being carried to Anomabu and held in the dungeons of a massive new fort, known today as Fort William, to await the arrival of ships like the *True Blue*. Their initial enslavement and imprisonment in Fort William were frightening and disorienting experiences, but once a ship arrived the real horror began.[2]

The voyage between West Africa and the New World was known as the Middle Passage and is infamous for the suffering and indignity it inflicted upon its victims. The entire Atlantic slave trade was a brutal business in which profit and loss were measured in human lives, but nowhere was this more evident than the Middle Passage. No trader wanted the slaves he was transporting to die crossing the Atlantic, but making them comfortable and keeping them healthy cost money, and if some died because a trader cut corners, that was considered the cost of doing business profitably. Thus, when slave ships anchored off Anomabu, men, women, and children were packed aboard them with barely enough room to move. Except for occasional opportunities to go on deck when the weather permitted it, they would then spend weeks packed in cramped, filthy spaces below deck. Providing them more room might have meant that more survived the journey, but packing them in provided a margin to cover the cost of those who died. Slave ships also took on food and water at Anomabu, but no captain wanted to carry any more than was absolutely necessary. Food and water took up space that might otherwise be used profitably to transport slaves, and any food or water left at the end of the voyage was money wasted. The goal was to take just enough for a speedy voyage; if the ship was delayed, rations could always be cut, or the number of mouths reduced by tossing some overboard.[3]

At the middle of the eighteenth century, 12 to 15 percent of the captives carried on slave ships travelling from the Gold Coast died during the Middle Passage. By that gruesome standard, the experience of those aboard the *True Blue* in 1759 was about average. Of the 280 captives taken on board at Anomabu, thirty-eight (13.6 percent) died before the ship reached Maryland. For those who survived the Middle Passage, the final days before their arrival typically involved the ship's crew trying to make them look as healthy and attractive as possible. They were washed, their skin might be oiled to give it a healthy sheen, and they might be given clean clothing—all in the hope that they would bring a better price when they were sold. Presumably, such a ritual took place aboard the *True Blue* before it docked. After it did, the Africans on board were taken ashore into an alien world. White people speaking a language they could not understand touched them, opened their mouths, and inspected them like they were cattle, and once the haggling and the bidding was over, they might be separated from the only family or friends they had left and taken by strangers on the road to an unknown fate at an unknown destination.[4]

Among the strangers inspecting captives unloaded from the *True Blue* in 1759 was William Preston. Born in Ireland in 1729, Preston had come to Virginia in 1738 when his family immigrated in search of better economic prospects. The family eventually settled in Augusta County, on the colony's western frontier, and there William came of age in a culture in which the two most critical components of economic success were land and labor. Land was relatively easy to acquire. Britain claimed sovereignty over millions of acres in western Virginia. Many of those acres, however, were inhabited by Native Americans loosely allied to the French, who were challenging British efforts to colonize the region. The British government, therefore, was anxious to evict the Native American population and to fill the land with new inhabitants loyal to Britain. To do so, colonial officials granted local speculators hundreds of thousands of acres of land on the condition that they settle a defined number of families on that land. The speculators then offered immigrants smaller tracts of land for free or for a modest annual quitrent until they had attracted enough settlers to meet the conditions of their grants while hoping to sell or lease the rest of the land to later arrivals at market prices and reap enormous profits. But acquiring land was only half of the challenge for a truly ambitious man. A single family could only cultivate a relatively small holding; to really make money, settlers needed additional workers in the form of servants or slaves.[5]

Enslaved workers were still relatively rare on the Virginia frontier at the time of the Prestons' arrival. Far more common were servants, especially indentured servants. Britain, Ireland, and the German states were home to thousands of families for whom America seemed to promise an escape from poverty, war, and religious persecution. Many of these families, however, lacked the resources to make a new start in America. They could pay neither the cost of a transatlantic voyage nor support themselves while they settled into their new lives in America. For many of them, indentured servitude offered an attractive solution. They could sign contracts—or indentures—agreeing to work for a specified number of years for the individual who paid their passage to America. This not only covered the cost of their transportation to America but also promised them board and upkeep while they adjusted to life in a new environment. Indentured servants were not slaves, and they enjoyed many of the civil and legal rights of other settlers. But they were legally bound to serve the terms spelled out in their contracts, and while the servants themselves could not be sold, their contracts and the legal right to their labor could be. Those with capital to invest or with access to credit could often buy servants' contracts at dockside from the shippers who had transported them, carry them onward to places where labor was in short supply, and resell their contracts for a profit.[6]

Such transactions were often made even more profitable by the head-rights attached to the servants. Since the early seventeenth century, many English colonies, including Virginia, had used land to entice individual settlers into the colony. Any immigrant who paid his or her own way to Virginia received a right to claim fifty acres of land from the colonial government. If a man brought his family, he received a similar headright for each member of the family, and early in Virginia's history, the government also began granting headrights to anyone transporting a servant or slave to the colony. As a result, speculators could not only make a profit buying and reselling slaves or the contracts of indentured servants, they could also claim the headrights attached to those slaves or servants and keep the land for themselves or sell it.

This was the economy and society in which William Preston grew up: one in which land and labor were commodities to be bought and sold and represented the surest route to financial, social, and political success. The young Preston gained an early understanding of this from his father, John, but his greatest opportunity came after John died in 1748, and William went to work for his uncle, James Patton. Patton by then was one of the most active and successful speculators and developers of land on the Virginia frontier and a powerful figure in the political elite of Augusta County, which then included almost all of Virginia west of the Blue Ridge. Preston served first as a clerk/assistant to his uncle in the latter's efforts to develop land along the New River, then known as Woods River. John Preston and James Patton had been among the founders of the Woods River Company, which in 1745 received a grant for one hundred thousand acres in south-west Virginia. To get the land, members of the company had to find families to settle it, and that meant providing those settlers with surveys and titles to the land they took up. This created a new opportunity for William Preston, and soon after joining the Woods River project he began an informal apprenticeship under Thomas Lewis, surveyor for Augusta County.[7]

County surveyors were men of tremendous importance on the Virginia frontier as their work was essential to orderly settlement of the region by British colonists. Theirs was also a position, however, from which the incumbent could profit significantly. County surveyors were among the first Europeans to see newly opened territory and could use that knowl-edge to claim valuable tracts of land for themselves. Preston became Lewis's

JUST ARRIVED *in* Patowmack *River from* AFRICA,

THE Ship TRUE BLUE, Captain WILLIAM RICE, with a Cargo of Three Hundred and Fifty choice healthy *Gold Coaſt* S L A V E S: The Sale of which will begin at *Nanjemoy*, on Monday the Twentieth Day of *Auguſt*, where due Attendance will be given, and continue till all are Sold.   JOHN CHAMPE & Company.

On August 16, 1759, the *Maryland Gazette* advertised the arrival of the *True Blue* and the sale of its cargo. (Collection of the Maryland State Archives)

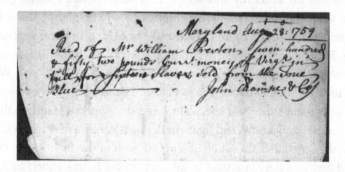

Receipt received by William Preston for the purchase of "sixteen slaves sold from the True Blue." (Library of Congress, Manuscript Division)

deputy in 1752 and spent the early 1750s surveying thousands of acres in the New River Valley. This not only provided a steady income but also gave him an intimate knowledge of land in the region that he quickly put to use for his own benefit. By 1754, Preston had acquired the rights to more than four thousand acres for himself, and like other enterprising Virginians of his day, he also began to invest in workers. By 1755 he had begun to purchase indentured servants to sell and to work his own land, and four years later he arrived at Nanjemoy Creek looking to buy his first slaves.[8]

This may have been Preston expanding the range of commodities in which he speculated: first land, then indentured servants, and now slaves. But 1759 is also the year in which Preston began buying the land that would become Greenfield, his first plantation, and he may have been looking for workers to use there. To find them Preston travelled to Nanjemoy, which in the 1750s was a convenient location for transatlantic slavers to land their cargoes because potential buyers from Virginia could easily cross the Potomac and avoid a 5 percent tax that Virginia imposed on the purchase of imported slaves. [9] It is impossible to say what Preston was looking for that day, or exactly what he bought, only that he paid John Champe & Company £752, Virginia currency, for "sixteen slaves sold from the True Blue." The amount Preston paid suggests that most of the people he bought that day were adults. The average price of an adult male slave on the Virginia frontier was £25 to £35, Virginia currency, in the 1750s and had risen to £55 to £70 by the early 1760s. Preston paid an average of £47 per head for the Africans he bought, which suggests that most of them were adults. Moreover, if Preston purchased any children and took them to back to Augusta County, Virginia law required him to present those children to the county court so the justices could estimate their ages for tax purposes. Preston did appear before the court in November of 1761 with a boy named Tom, judged to be twelve years old, who may have been one of those purchased at Nanjemoy, but it is impossible to be certain. All that is known for sure is that on August 28, 1759, William Preston bought sixteen enslaved Africans who had recently arrived aboard the *True Blue*.[10]

Preston continued buying and selling enslaved workers for the rest of his life. Some he purchased from neighbors, and these may have been second or third generation Virginians. Others he bought from Tidewater merchants, and these may have just arrived from the Caribbean or directly from Africa. Some of the people he bought purely as commodities and quickly sold them on to other buyers. Others were longer-term investments he lent or leased to tenants renting land from him. At least some of the enslaved workers he bought, however, came to live and work at Preston's estate, Greenfield, in what is now Botetourt County. By the early 1770s, Greenfield had grown to more than twelve hundred acres on which Preston's workers raised cattle, corn and other grains, flax, and hemp. There was also an orchard and a distillery on the property. Much of the work involved in these activities was performed by enslaved men and women—at least sixteen by 1773—under the supervision of a White overseer. Preston, himself, was ultimately in charge, but his duties as a surveyor, militia officer, and local politician meant that he probably had little to do with day-to-day operations at Greenfield. [11]

Survey work, in particular, consumed a significant portion of Preston's time. He served as deputy surveyor of Augusta County from 1752 until 1770, and when Botetourt County was carved out of western Augusta in 1770, he was appointed county surveyor of the new jurisdiction. In both of these positions, Preston's duties meant that he came to spend more and more time in the New River Valley. At the middle of the eighteenth century, the New River Valley was an ideal place for speculators to operate because it lay at a geographic and human crossroads. In the late 1720s, thousands of English, German, and Scots-Irish immigrants had begun moving south and west out of Pennsylvania in search of land and opportunity. They did so via the Great Appalachian Valley, which brought them, first, to the Shenandoah Valley and then to the James and Roanoke River Valleys. Along the way, they merged with a second human tide coming from the east. Rivers such as the Potomac, the James, and the Roanoke led migrants out of eastern Virginia, through the Blue Ridge Mountains, and into the Appalachian Valley. Together, these two streams of humanity began flowing into the New River Valley during the late 1740s and early 1750s. Settlement slowed dramatically during the French and Indian War (1755–63), when attacks by Native Americans destroyed several settlements in the region, including one at Draper's Meadow that William Preston and James Patton were visiting at the time, but by the early 1760s the danger had passed and settlement in the watershed of the New River accelerated rapidly, in spite of British efforts to restrict it.[12]

William Preston had been surveying land in the New River Valley since the early 1750s and by the early 1770s had come to own considerable acreage there himself. By then, European settlement and the business of surveying land was expanding westward, and Preston came to see that Greenfield would soon be inconveniently distant from the focus of that business. As a result, early in the 1770s Preston purchased several contiguous tracts of land along Stroubles Creek, a tributary of the New River that flowed down a broad valley running from east to west across what is now Montgomery County. This land would soon become the core of Preston's new homeplace, Smithfield, and on it he set out to establish a plantation complex that would demonstrate and perpetuate his family's position among the local elite.[13]

In eighteenth-century Virginia, members of the colonial elite—the gentry—were expected to demonstrate their place in society through conspicuous economic signals. They had to dress, live, and entertain lavishly, and

central to these displays of wealth were houses befitting their status as gen-
tlemen. Smithfield was intended to be just such a house. It was far more
elegant than the log structure Preston inhabited at Greenfield and was built
in the Georgian style favored by Virginia's Tidewater elite. The main house
was a frame structure with one and a half stories above a brick basement,
and its interior was marked by finely carved mantles, molding, and stair
rails similar to those found in Williamsburg. Surrounding the main house
were a number of outbuildings that supported its domestic life and contributed to what one historian called "the gentry's landscape." Though modest
by Tidewater standards, Smithfield was larger and more stylish than anything else in the neighborhood. It was a mansion, clearly meant to symbol-
ize the Prestons' position as New River aristocracy, and by early 1774 it was
finished enough to occupy.[14]

To maintain a house like Smithfield and the lifestyle it embodied required
an equally impressive income. Preston's role as the county surveyor provided part of that income, but the rest would have to come from the hundreds of acres of land surrounding the house. Making that land productive,
however, required enormous amounts of labor, most of it provided by
enslaved Africans or African Americans. First, they had to clear the land,
which took months of backbreaking labor. Small sections may have been
previously cleared by Native Americans or by earlier settlers, but much of
the land surrounding Smithfield was still wooded when Preston acquired it.
Clearing it involved felling thousands of trees and gathering them into piles
to burn. Then, using oxen, workers had to pull tree stumps out of the ground
and level the disrupted landscape their removal created. Only then could
they begin to develop pastures for Preston's livestock and fields for his crops,
build fences to keep the livestock out of the crops, and erect the barns, sheds,
slave quarters, and other outbuildings essential to a functioning plantation.
And, of course, once the work of establishing the plantation was done, it had
to be operated and maintained.

As it had been at Greenfield, hemp was the principal cash crop raised
at Smithfield. During the years of the American Revolution, demand for
local hemp rose dramatically as Virginia and the United States each raised
military and naval forces that needed rope. Preston was able to sell all the
hemp Smithfield could produce through Edward Johnson, the brother-in-
law of his wife and a merchant based in Manchester, Virginia. Johnson had
been buying hemp from Preston since 1769, at least, but as the demand

for military supplies rose, Johnson invested in a ropewalk and let Preston know that he would buy all the hemp Preston could provide. Preston also continued to make and sell whiskey, as he had at Greenfield, and this business also expanded during the latter half of the 1770s. In addition to hemp and whiskey produced for market, Smithfield produced a variety of crops for sale or for the Prestons' own use—including flax, wheat, rye, barley, oats, corn, potatoes, turnips, and hay—as well as cattle. And nearly all of the labor involved in producing these crops was that of enslaved workers.[15]

With the establishment of Smithfield, Preston seems to have increased the pace at which he purchased indentured servants and slaves, and the relative balance between the two shifted toward the latter as the Revolution reduced trade with England and made servants increasingly scarce. Moreover, more of the workers Preston bought seem to have been for his own use rather than for resale. By the time William Preston died in 1783, Smithfield included almost two thousand acres of land, and the variety of crops raised there all required labor. Hemp production, in particular, involved several stages that were highly labor-intensive. Seedbeds were often plowed or harrowed two or three times in order to break up the soil prior to seeding, and then they were seeded twice or three times to ensure that enough seed germinated. The harvest and its aftermath were even more demanding. Ripe hemp plants were pulled from the earth, not cut, because the bottom few inches of the stalks were especially productive. Then the stalks were tied in bundles and propped up to dry. Next, the dried hemp had to be "rotted"—either by soaking in a creek or pond for several days or lying in a field through the winter months. This allowed moisture and fermentation to separate the thin layer of hemp fibers from the outer bark of the plant and from its woody core. After rotting, the flax was dried again and then "broken," which involved placing the stalks in a pair of hinged jaws—a break—and applying just enough pressure to shatter the woody bark and core without breaking the fibers. Finally, the broken stalks were whipped against the break to dislodge fragments of the bark and core and leave the fiber clean and ready for use. [16]

Hemp was the chief market crop produced at Smithfield during its first decade, and it did involve significant labor, but it was hardly the only demand on workers' time. Grain fields needed to be plowed and sown and the resulting crops harvested; hay needed to be mowed and stacked; and livestock needed at least some care, even if herds were often left to fend for themselves. There were also new fields to be cleared, fences and buildings to be maintained, and a variety other tasks necessary to support such a large agricultural enterprise. And at least some of those enslaved at Smithfield performed nonagricultural tasks as well. Family tradition among the Prestons maintains that some of the furniture at Smithfield was built by enslaved artisans, and William Preston arranged for at least one of his enslaved workers to train as a weaver. In addition, the Preston family continued to enjoy a relatively luxurious lifestyle supported by numerous cooks and domestic workers.[17]

To meet these multiple demands, Preston more than doubled the number of enslaved workers he held between 1773 and 1782. By the latter year, he owned thirty-four in Montgomery County alone and was the largest slave owner in the county. Preston may still have been buying and selling slaves as commodities during these years, but the thirty-four identified in 1782 seem to have been an established workforce at Smithfield and those workers' children. Each was identified by first name on the 1782 tax roll, and thirty-two of the thirty-four individuals named that year also appear on the 1783 list of Preston's taxable property. Moreover, twenty-three of the thirty-four named in 1783 subsequently appear among the enslaved individuals distributed among Preston's heirs early in the next century. Unfortunately, it is impossible to say with certainty how long any of those enslaved at Smithfield in 1783 had been with Preston. Almost certainly some of the adults named on the 1783 tax list were old enough to have arrived aboard the *True Blue*, but the tax list does not provide their exact ages, only that they were over the age of twenty-one in 1783. One name on the list, Jack, certainly raises the possibility that he had been among the sixteen kidnapped Africans purchased by William Preston in 1759. Preston owned a man named Jack as early as 1762, and if that Jack is the same man as the Jack named among Preston's taxable property in 1783, then he may well have been one of those who arrived aboard the *True Blue*.[18]

The tax lists also provide a glimpse of the age and sex distribution of the enslaved community at Smithfield in the early 1780s and of family formation in that community. All of the names on the tax rolls seem to be typical male or female names such as Ned and Jack or Fanny and Nelly. Based on those names, the enslaved population at Smithfield in 1782–83 was skewed noticeably toward males; in 1782 males represented twenty of Preston's thirty-four enslaved workers, and in 1783 they were nineteen of thirty-four.

The 1783 list also indicates whether an individual was under the age of sixteen, over the age of twenty-one, or between sixteen and twenty-one. In that year, at least, fifteen of those enslaved at Smithfield were aged sixteen and over, while nineteen were younger than sixteen. Combining the names and ages indicates that the gender balance was somewhat closer among those sixteen and older (eight males and seven females) than among those younger than sixteen (eleven males and eight females). Thus, it was demographically possible, at least, that most of the enslaved adults at Smithfield could have found marriage partners on the plantation, though it is impossible to say how many actually did.[19]

The tax lists also suggest that by 1783 children were being born at Smithfield and that at least some of the people enslaved there were members of families. Evidence of children being born at Smithfield lies in the fact that between 1782 and 1783 two new names—Judy and Esther—appeared on the tax list and that both individuals were under the age of sixteen. It is possible that Preston purchased two female children that year, but it seems more likely they were born on the plantation. The tax lists also strongly suggest that by 1782–83 the enslaved population at Smithfield included at least some families. Both Primus and Jem appear among the names of males over the age of twenty-one and those under the age of sixteen, which suggests that they represent father and son pairs. Moreover, those named on the 1783 tax roll include an adult woman named Silvia, a boy named Peter, and a girl named Cynthia. In 1816, William Preston's daughter, Letitia, and her husband, John Floyd, purchased from her father's estate a group that included Silvy ("old"), Peter (age thirty-five), Cynthia (age thirty-eight), and Silvy (age two). The names and ages in this group suggest that Peter or Cynthia was the child of "Old" Silvy that they had married between 1783 and 1816 and that they had a daughter, Silvy, named for her grandmother.[20]

Collectively, the men and women enslaved at Smithfield were still in the process of creating their own distinctive community. Preston's first enslaved workers had all been Africans, but that does not mean they were a homogenous group. Captives brought to Anomabu and transferred to ships like the *True Blue* came from a variety of West African linguistic and ethnic groups. They spoke a variety of languages, organized their families and communities in a variety of ways, and worshipped a variety of gods. The sixteen Africans William Preston bought in 1759 may have shared some common characteristics, but they almost certainly represented an array of cultures and languages. Some of them may have spoken the same or mutually intelligible languages, but others may have initially been unable to communicate with anyone around them. And, of course, none of them spoke English, and none of them were familiar with the Anglo-American world in which they found themselves after leaving Anomabu. In the months and years following their arrival in Virginia they had learned to communicate in an alien language, to dress and behave in ways their owners thought appropriate, and to work in ways that were often unlike anything they had known in Africa. As for the men and women Preston acquired after 1759, it is impossible to say who they were. They may also have been Africans, from cultures similar to, or different from, those carried aboard the *True Blue*, or they may have been born and raised in Virginia or another British colony.

First at Greenfield and then at Smithfield, Preston's enslaved workers forged new ways of living that combined elements of the African and British worlds they remembered or had come to know. Not surprisingly, the elements of that life most visible to the Preston family probably reflected the dominant White culture. There is, for example, no evidence of any housing for those enslaved at Smithfield except for the sort of log cabins built by so many European colonists in America. Thus, it seems safe to conclude that these first workers enslaved at Smithfield also lived in log structures—either dedicated quarters or spaces in various domestic outbuildings such as the summer kitchen. The clothing and food they received was also more likely to be Euro-American than African. William Preston left no record describing how he clothed or fed his workers, but it seems likely that they wore the same type of basic "negro clothing" found throughout the colony and lived on rations of corn and pork supplemented by whatever they could catch or grow on their own. In those parts of their lives that were less visible to the Prestons though, these first enslaved workers at Smithfield seem to have retained some features of the African cultures from which they originally came. As described more fully in chapter 3, enslaved workers at Smithfield often marked significant events in their lives by gathering at a large white oak in what seems to have been an echo of West African cultural and religious practices. They may also have continued to employ African names among themselves, although Preston gave them all English names immediately after he acquired them. Almost certainly they continued to tell African stories and sing African songs in the relative privacy of the quarters in which they lived, and they may even have preserved some of their traditional funeral practices. No graves of enslaved workers have yet been discovered at Smithfield, but as burials could occur beyond the Prestons' view, the enslaved may have been able to maintain some of their traditional practices.[21]

Through the work of these men and women, Smithfield took shape in the decade following its establishment. By the time William Preston died, in June 1783, he owned more than twenty thousand acres spread across several Virginia counties, including some in what would later become Kentucky; more than two hundred head of livestock; and forty-two enslaved people, and he left very precise instructions for dividing this extensive estate among his widow and their eleven surviving children. The land that was Smithfield remained intact and would remain essentially intact until after the Civil War. Preston's will stipulated that following his death the ownership of Smithfield would depend on where his widow, Susanna, chose to live. Susanna was expected to live with her son James Patton Preston, so James was to inherit either Greenfield or Smithfield, depending on where his mother chose to live. Ultimately, Susanna elected to remain at Smithfield, and its title eventually passed to James, but because he had just turned nine when his father died, Susanna continued to oversee the plantation until he came of age. In his turn, James Patton Preston owned and occupied Smithfield until his death in 1843, when it passed to his four surviving children. Each of his three sons—William, Robert, and James Preston—operated a separate plantation on a portion of the land, though it was not formally divided until 1865. Their sister, Catharine, also received a share of Smithfield, but she died just a few years after her father, and her widower, who had his own plantation in Pittsylvania County, sold Catharine's share to her brothers in 1852.[22]

For the enslaved residents of Smithfield, the situation was more complicated. William Preston left to his widow "the use & profit of all my plantations, slaves & stock of every kind" but also directed that "when any of my daughters are married or my sons of age or married" Susanna was to give her or him "such part of my slaves & stock or money in lieu thereof as she with the advice & council of any two of my executors under their hands thinks just & reasonable so as neither to straiten herself or do the least injustice to my other children." In fact, few of those enslaved by William Preston passed to any of his children for more than twenty years. Nine of the thirty-four individuals named as taxable property of William Preston in

1783 seem to have died or run away or to have been sold or transferred to one of the heirs during that time, but the rest remained together at Smithfield, where additional births increased their number to fifty-one by 1806. During the next decade, though, heirs of William Preston met twice to divide his estate—including his human property—and many of the people enslaved at Smithfield since the 1780s left for new homes elsewhere in Virginia or in Kentucky.[23]

The first division took place in September 1806, when William Preston's heirs or their representatives gathered at Smithfield to negotiate "an amicable adjustment & final settlement of the estate of the said William Preston." The only known source detailing the outcome of this agreement is a series of lists compiled by Francis Preston, one of the heirs participating in the exercise. Unfortunately, the lists sometimes contradict one another. Fifteen individuals included on a list of "Negroes retained by my mother," for example, are also among the thirty-one named on "a list of the negroes given up by my mother." Comparing the 1806 lists to records from later distributions of the estate seems to show that Susanna Preston retained sixteen enslaved people in 1806. These individuals remained at Smithfield, along with seven others allotted to James Patton Preston, while the remaining twenty-nine identified as part of the estate of William Preston were divided among his ten other surviving children and dispersed to new homes in Kentucky or western Virginia.[24]

The decade following the 1806 agreement saw continued growth of the enslaved population at Smithfield as at least five children were born to women Susanna had retained in the division of her husband's estate. The 1810 federal census reported that Susanna owned twenty slaves, and by 1816 the number had grown to at least twenty-four. Susanna Preston, however, was growing old. By 1816, she was seventy-seven, and according to her son, Francis, she was "too old to manage her negroes." As a result, the surviving heirs or their representatives met again at Smithfield that October to negotiate another division of Smithfield's enslaved population. This time Susanna retained five or six individuals for her personal use: John Fraction; William Dandridge; a woman named Suckey and her daughter, Martha; and another woman, Flora, who may also have had a child. Eighteen others were to be allocated to or sold among the other heirs of William Preston. If possible, the heirs wished to allocate the eighteen among themselves, but "if a division & allotment cannot be agreed upon" they were to be sold to the highest bidder among the heirs. The new owners were then to pay annually a percentage of the appraised value or purchase price of those they acquired sufficient to provide Susanna with an income of $250 each year until her death. Ultimately, the heirs could not agree on a plan to divide the eighteen, and they were sold to James McDowell and John Floyd, each of whom was married to a daughter of William and Susanna Preston.[25]

A final division of William Preston's estate, and a further scattering of his enslaved workers, came with the death of Susanna Preston in 1823. At the time of her death, Susanna still held the four adults she had retained in 1816—John Fraction, William Dandridge, Flora, and Suckey—as well as four of the women's children. Suckey had one daughter, Martha in 1816 and since then, had given birth to two more, Edmonia and Frances. Flora also had a child by the time Susanna Preston died, though it is unclear whether that child was born before or after 1816. All eight of these individuals were sold to heirs of William Preston. Suckey and her daughters were purchased by Elizabeth Preston Madison and moved to her home near Shawsville, in eastern Montgomery County, while Flora and her child were taken to what is now Pulaski County by John and Letitia Preston Floyd. William Dandridge and John Fraction, however, were purchased by James Patton Preston and remained at Smithfield with some thirty others Preston owned by then, most of whom he had acquired on his own rather than through inheritance.[26]

In the course of these various divisions, the Prestons may have kept some enslaved families together. In 1816, for example, James McDowell, the husband of William Preston's daughter Sarah, purchased from the estate Jack (age thirty-three), Chloe (age thirty), Nanny (age six or seven),Thomas (age four), and Judy (age nine). The structure and ages of this group suggest that Nanny and Thomas, and perhaps Judy, were the children of Jack and Chloe and that part of their family, at least, remained together when its members were sold and taken to Rockbridge County by the McDowells. At the same time, Letitia Preston Floyd and her husband, John, seem to have purchased a multigenerational family consisting of Peter (age thirty-five), Cynthia, (age thirty-eight), Silvy (age two), Ruben (age five), Lucy (age four), and "Old" Silvia. In other cases, though, families seem to have been divided. In 1802, for example, William Preston's daughter Margaret married her second cousin, John Preston, and moved to his home in Washington County. Either at the time of her marriage, as her father's will directed, or in the 1806 division described above, Margaret received a number of people held at Smithfield and moved them to her new home in Abingdon. Based on the names of freedpeople living in Washington and Montgomery Counties after the Civil War, it seems that Margaret took with her at least some members of the Fraction family, while other members of the family remained at Smithfield. Naming patterns also suggest that members of the Fraction family may have gone with Sarah Preston McDowell to Rockbridge County and with Susanna Preston Hart to Kentucky.[27]

By the time Susanna Preston died, the enslaved population at Smithfield had changed significantly since the days of William Preston. Nearly all of the individuals held by William Preston at the time of his death had died or been distributed among his heirs and taken to other plantations in Virginia or Kentucky, as had many of their children and grandchildren. And the new master of Smithfield, James Patton Preston, had acquired additional workers on his own. By 1826 he held at least thirty-nine people in bondage at Smithfield—more than his father ever had.[28] Some of those held by James Patton Preston definitely seem to have been the descendants of men and women acquired by his father, but few of those held at Smithfield in 1826 can be identified that conclusively. During the next several decades, though, Smithfield's enslaved community continued to grow, and as it did specific individuals and families within that population begin to emerge more clearly.

❖ 2 ❖

The Enslaved People of Smithfield

In seeking to identify more precisely the individuals and families enslaved at Smithfield, the best starting point is the death of James Patton Preston. Following Preston's death, in May 1843, his administrators compiled a detailed inventory of his estate, including ninety-one enslaved men, women, and children he owned when he died.[1] This inventory includes the name of each individual, his or her age at the time, and his or her estimated market value. Few of those on the inventory are identified with surnames, and many people today assume from such documents that most slaves had no last names. In fact, a variety of documents shows that most slaves did have surnames, even if Whites generally chose to ignore them. Comparing groups of names on the inventory to groups found on other records that include surnames or details of relationships shows that many of the names on the inventory of James Patton Preston's estate are organized by family. This makes it possible to identify the individual members of those families, and by looking at records produced before and after 1843, it is often possible to reconstruct their life histories. Of the ninety-one names on the inventory, forty-seven can be identified with confidence as specific individuals. In addition, a number of children born after 1843 to women on the list can also be identified from later records and connected to their families.

In reconstructing the enslaved community at Smithfield, it is also important to look beyond the particular tract of land known today as Smithfield. Following the death of James Patton Preston, his three sons operated three separate plantations on what had been their father's estate. William Ballard

The inventory of James Patton Preston's estate identified ninety-one enslaved men, women, and children by name, age, and appraised value. (Clerk of the Court, Montgomery County, Virginia)

Preston continued to occupy the central portion of the original plantation, which retained the name Smithfield; Robert T. Preston lived on the eastern portion of his father's land on a plantation named Solitude; and James F. Preston established White Thorn on the western third of the original Smithfield. Each son also received a number of the people enslaved by their father, as did his daughter, Catharine Jane Preston, who married George H. Gilmer in 1845 and moved with her property to Gilmer's home in Pittsylvania County. So far, fifty-eight of the ninety-one individuals named on the inventory can be followed at the division of James Patton Preston's estate: twenty of the fifty-eight went to William Ballard, seventeen to Robert, fifteen to James, and six to Catharine. Wherever they went, though, all ninety-one of those named on the inventory are included among those enslaved at Smithfield for the purpose of this study, as are their spouses and children—even if they never actually lived at Smithfield. In addition, a number of individuals held by the sons of James Patton Preston before their father's death or acquired afterwards can also be identified, and they too are included in Smithfield's enslaved community.[2]

Between 1774 and 1865 the number of people enslaved at greater Smithfield grew significantly, in spite of the estate divisions described earlier. When William Preston died in 1783, there were thirty-four enslaved individuals at Smithfield. By 1843, when James Patton Preston died, that number had nearly tripled, to ninety-one, and it continued growing until slavery at Smithfield ended. The federal census of 1860, the last to include slaves, reported that the three Preston plantations that had been part of the original Smithfield held a total of 106 people in slavery: 50 at Smithfield, 33 at Solitude, and 23 at White Thorn. In addition, perhaps a dozen more with links to Smithfield were living on George H. Gilmer's plantation in Pittsylvania County.[3]

Some of this growth came through the purchase of additional workers. Family correspondence from the early nineteenth century indicates that the children of William Preston frequently bought and sold slaves as they sought to establish their own plantations in Virginia and Kentucky, though they do not seem to have bought them quite as frequently as their father had. Nor do they seem to have purchased them as speculative investments. Writing from Smithfield in 1801, William Preston Jr. described a recent conversation with a "Col. Brown" about "the negro business." William was trying to decide whether or not to attend an upcoming sale in Bedford County at which fifty enslaved people were to be sold. "The thing is profitable" he wrote, "but the risque is great so that I have not yet come to a determination what to do." The family did, however, continue buying and selling African Americans for long as it was legal to do so. William Ballard Preston, for example, bought a woman named Nancy in 1856, and his estate sold two enslaved adults, John Smith and a woman named Sidney in

1863.[4] Others came to the Prestons through marriage. In 1839, William Ballard Preston married Lucinda Staples Redd, who as the only child of Waller Redd, had inherited land and slaves in Henry County at the death of her father in 1825. Through his wife, Preston owned at least 150 enslaved people in Henry County and, over the years, may have brought some of them to Montgomery County. Similarly, when James F. Preston married Sarah Anne Caperton in 1855, his bride seems to have come to White Thorn with a number of men and women she had inherited from her father.[5]

Smithfield's enslaved population also grew naturally as enslaved women gave birth to enslaved children. Some of these children may have been the offspring of their masters. Historians have long known that slave owners often took advantage of their position to sexually exploit female slaves. Mary Boykin Chestnut, the wife of a South Carolina planter, famously described the results of this power imbalance in her diary: "like the patriarchs of old, our men live all in one house with their wives and their concubines; and the mulattos one sees in every family partly resemble the white children."[6] None of the Preston women are known to have expressed such views, but the descendants of those enslaved at Smithfield did preserve stories that their ancestors were the offspring of Preston men. William McNorton, for example, was described as light-skinned, and after his death it was reported that he had claimed to be the son of his master and an enslaved woman. In fact, William McNorton was not born until 1867, two years after slavery ended in Virginia, but the reports of his mixed ancestry could have been a jumbled reference to William's father, Orville McNorton, who was born at Smithfield in 1841.[7]

Most of the children born at Smithfield, however, were probably the result of unions between enslaved men and women on the plantation. No slave marriage in Virginia had any legal standing, but owners like the Prestons often believed that marriage and family were valuable institutions to encourage among their workers. Many owners hoped that the emotional ties a family created would help keep those they held in bondage from trying to escape. Running away with children was much more difficult than doing so alone, and the thought of leaving a spouse behind might deter a potential escapee. Simple economics also motivated slave owners to encourage family formation. Any children born to enslaved women were legally the property of those women's owners and represented future workers the owners could employ or assets they could sell.[8]

The fact that masters encouraged it, however, did nothing to reduce the importance of marriage or families to enslaved men and women themselves. They saw families as a valuable source of emotional and physical support and as important weapons in their battle against the dehumanizing effects of slavery. To enslaved men and women, family formation, even in the restricted form available to them, was a sign of their humanity.[9] And whatever the law said, enslaved couples in Montgomery County considered their unions just as legitimate as those of White couples. Thomas and Lucy Fuqua, for example, had married in August 1864 while both were still enslaved. A decade later, Lucy sought a divorce on the grounds that Thomas had formed "an adulterous connection" with another women. In the course of the proceedings, one of the witnesses in the case was asked if the couple had been "lawfully married after the surrender." He replied, "they was lawfully married before the surrender by their master's word." Such comments make it clear that even without legal sanction marriages between enslaved men and women were valued and respected by those who entered them and by the communities in which they lived.[10]

Naming patterns also seem to demonstrate the importance of family among those enslaved by the Prestons. Before 1826, few of the individuals enslaved at Smithfield can be linked to their siblings, spouses, or children, so one could conclude that the repetition of names such as Primus, Silvy, Reuben, and Flora between 1780 and 1820 was a coincidence. Nor is it possible to say who chose these names. It may have been the enslaved themselves, but it could have been their enslavers instead. After 1826, however, a number of the families enslaved at Smithfield can be reconstructed across multiple generations over almost two-hundred years. In these families, it is abundantly clear that particular names were often repeated within particular families and that they were selected by family members and not by the Prestons. Montreville, Walter, Emily, Catherine, and Grace were repeated over several generations of McNortons, as were Virginia and Wilson among the Fractions, and Saunders among the Moons. In some cases children were named after a parent or grandparent, but others were named after an aunt or uncle. A number of other names, including Granville, Chloe, and Othello, appear before and after 1826, which suggests that these names were also repeated within families, though the absence of information regarding relationships before 1826 makes it impossible to say for sure.[11]

Enslaved families took a variety of forms. Some, especially those on larger plantations, were nuclear families in which the husband, wife, and children all lived together in the same home. Other families, however, were not the male-headed, nuclear units that White observers associated with the term. Slavery and the property rights of slave owners often made it impossible for the enslaved to establish or to maintain such families. Many owners held too few adults to provide marriage partners for all of their workers, or the gender ratio on a particular farm might be too unbalanced to support traditional nuclear families. Such situations often led to "abroad marriages" in which the partners belonged to different owners. These couples might spend most of their time living apart and see one another only on Sundays and holidays. Even when it was possible for men and women enslaved on the same holding to marry one another and establish families that lived together, their situation could easily change. Their marriages had no legal standing, and slave owners had the unquestioned legal right to separate couples or to take children from their parents at any time and for any reason. As a result, enslaved families were often headed by women whose partners visited their wives and children if they could, and in the absence of immediate blood or marital kin, such families often relied more on extended family connections—siblings and grandparents—or on fictive kin—"aunts," "uncles," and "grannies" who were not actually related—than White families did.[12]

Two different documents help to capture the structure of enslaved families at Smithfield. The first is the 1843 inventory of the estate of James Patton Preston. On it, individuals seem to have been grouped by families: couples followed by their children and women without resident partners followed by their children. The picture is incomplete, though, because it offers no evidence concerning the status of men at Smithfield who may have had wives and children on other farms. A second snapshot comes from Montgomery County's cohabitation register, compiled by the Freedmen's Bureau in 1866. Because antebellum Virginia law made no provision for any African American marriage, either slave or free, the abolition of slavery meant that thousands of newly freed couples faced a situation in which neither their marriages nor their children had any legal standing. Under pressure from federal officials, Virginia established a mechanism in 1866 to legitimize Black marriages and births. Officials of the Freedmen's Bureau—the federal office charged with protecting the welfare of freedpeople in the former Confederate states—invited any African American couple "cohabiting together" to register their union and any children born of it. Not all couples learned of this possibility in time to register, not all of those who did learn of it wanted to register, and not all of those who wanted to register were able to do so. Thus, Montgomery County's cohabitation register also contains only a sample of the enslaved couples who had married there, and it is impossible to say how large or small that sample is.[13]

While neither the inventory nor the cohabitation register provides a complete picture of enslaved families at Smithfield, they do make clear that marriage and family formation were common among those enslaved at Smithfield during the nineteenth century. Preston's inventory, for example, seems to include evidence of nine couples or women and their children. Of the ninety-one individuals named on the inventory of James Patton Preston's estate, fifty-six appear to have been members of one of these units. Among them are examples of each of the family types common among those enslaved in the antebellum United States: resident couples in which the couple lived together on the same farm or plantation; abroad marriages, in which the husband and wife lived on different farms; enslaved women with children but with no known partners; and couples in which one partner was enslaved and the other a free person of color.

Among the resident couples at Smithfield in 1843, for example, were John and Easther Fraction. John Fraction was born about 1800 and seems to have been the second or third generation of that family enslaved by the Prestons. He first appears in the historical record as "Jack's John" and seems to have been either the son or grandson of the Jack identified earlier as, perhaps, one of the original sixteen Africans William Preston purchased off the *True Blue* in 1759.[14] His wife, Easther, was also born about 1800 and also seems to have been born at Smithfield. She was, perhaps, the daughter of a girl named Esther, who also appears on William Preston's 1783 tax list, but that cannot be confirmed.[15] The histories of another married couple at Smithfield, William and Catherine McNorton, are less clear. They too were born about 1800 and may be the Billy and Caty who appear among the individuals who passed to James Patton Preston when the estate of William Preston was divided in 1806. Like John Fraction, William and Catherine McNorton may have been born to parents who were already enslaved by the Prestons, but they may have been purchased by the estate as children or purchased by James Patton Preston himself, and never been part of his father's estate.[16]

It is also uncertain when either the Fractions or the McNortons married, though the first children known to have been born to them were born about 1819 (Marsha McNorton) and 1821 (Mary Fraction). In 1843, both couples were living as Smithfield with at least some of their children and grandchildren. William and Cate McNorton appear on the inventory of James Patton Preston with thirteen children between the ages of one and twenty-four. John and Easther Fraction appear with ten children between the ages of two and twenty-two, and subsequent records indicate that the Fractions had at least two more children after 1843. The inventory also reveals that two of the McNortons' daughters, Marsha and Eliza, and the Fractions' daughter Mary each had a young child of her own. Later records and oral histories indicate that Marsha McNorton was married to an enslaved man named Frank Sanders and her sister, Eliza, to a man named Rubin Burke.[17] Neither of these men appear in any surviving records from Smithfield, so these may have been abroad marriages, though it is impossible to be sure. In the case of Mary Fraction, all that is known is that on the inventory her name is followed immediately by that of one-year-old Daniel Jones. This suggests that Daniel was Mary's son by a man named Jones, though who he was and what the precise nature of their relationship was remains unknown.

Also living at Smithfield in 1843 was the family of Peggy Saunders. Peggy, or Margaret as she identified herself in 1866, was born Margaret Dandridge about 1801 and was probably born at Smithfield. The 1826 list of enslaved people belonging to the estate of William Preston and retained by Susanna until her death includes "one negro man William Dandridge," which suggests that the Dandridge family had been at Smithfield since the days of William Preston. Margaret Dandridge had married Richard Saunders in 1825, and it seems to have been an abroad marriage in which the couple enjoyed occasional visits but did not live together. The 1843 inventory includes Margaret and ten children between the ages of one and seventeen but not Richard. Richard and Margaret Saunders do appear together, however, on the 1866 cohabitation register, on which Richard identified his last owner as William Henderson of Botetourt County.[18]

One other family can be identified by name on the 1843 inventory, that of William and Louisa Moon, but it is visible only through the couple's children. Among those named on the inventory are Hiram, Preston, Saunders, and Francis Moon—the sons of William and Louisa Moon.[19] Neither of their parents is named, though, because by 1843 Louisa was probably dead, and William was what Virginia law called a "free negro."

By the early nineteenth century, free people of color had long been a small and awkward element of Virginia's population. When the first African captives arrived at Jamestown, White Virginians had no experience with slavery and no laws defining it. As a result, at least some of these first Africans regained their freedom after completing terms of service. They and their descendants formed the nucleus of a small, modestly successful community of free Blacks in colonial Virginia. That community continued to grow slowly during the seventeenth and early eighteenth centuries, augmented by descendants of those original free Black families and by the mixed-race children of Black male slaves and White female indentured servants. The number of free Blacks then grew rapidly for a quarter century after the American Revolution as a result of a 1782 law that permitted individual owners in Virginia to manumit—set free—their slaves. Indeed, their number grew so significantly after 1782 that in 1806, in the wake of the Haitian Revolution and Gabriel's Rebellion, the General Assembly amended the law to require that any Virginia slave manumitted after 1806 leave the state within a year unless granted permission to stay by the legislature (later changed to the court of the county in which he or she lived). This did lead some of those manumitted after 1806 to emigrate, and it did slow significantly the rate of growth in Virginia's free people of color, but that population continued to grow through the final decades of the antebellum era.[20]

Virginia law also restricted sharply what free people of color in Virginia were allowed to do. Some restrictions had applied since the colonial period—denial of the vote, for example, and the 1782 law permitting private manumissions allowed the arrest of "any emancipated slave travelling out of the county of his or her residence without a copy of the instrument of his or her emancipation." During the early nineteenth century, however, the range of restrictions increased significantly. New laws required free people of color to register with the court of the city or county in which they lived and to renew their registrations regularly, forbid them to possess firearms, forbid them to preach or to attend any religious service conducted by a slave or a free person of color without White supervision, and forbid them to attend school. The enforcement of these laws was far from universal, though. Laws curtailing the actions of free Blacks and mulattos *as a group* appealed to White Virginians' racial anxiety, but they were frequently ignored in *individual* cases involving free Blacks familiar in a particular community and trusted by their neighbors. As a result, many free people of color in antebellum Virginia managed to carve out niches for themselves in the particular communities in which they lived—including Montgomery County.[21]

It is impossible to say when the first free people of color arrived in Montgomery County, but it certainly happened before 1790 because the federal census that year counted six "other free persons" in the county's population. Over the next seventy years, that number rose steadily, though it remained fairly small. By 1860 the number had reached 147: less than 2 percent of the county's total free population that year and just over 6 percent of its total Black or mulatto population. Because manumission usually generated a public record, and no such records have been found from Montgomery County before the nineteenth century, it seems that the county's first free people of color probably migrated there. Despite laws intended to deter them, they continued to migrate into Montgomery County during the antebellum years and did so until at least the eve of the Civil War, if not beyond. Manumission did add to their number, though. Between 1803 and 1860, at least eighty-two enslaved residents of Montgomery County were freed by their owners, and though many of these left the county, as many as twelve of the eighty-two may have settled there. One of these was William Moon.

William Moon was born about 1785 in Montgomery County. Nothing is known of his early life, but as an adult, he was enslaved by Jacob Price. Prices were among the earliest settlers in what would become Montgomery County and gave their name to the community of Prices Fork, two miles west of Smithfield. Most of the Prices were middling farmers who rarely owned slaves. A few members of the family did hold enslaved workers, though, and Jacob Price owned at least one: a man he called Bill or Billy. Early census records indicate that Jacob Price held one enslaved male, and in 1834 Price included "a negro man slave named Bill" in the property he used to guarantee a debt of $563.55 to William Ballard Preston. Price must have repaid the debt because three years later, in 1837, he freed Bill "in consideration of a sense of justice, gratitude and high personal regard, and in consideration of faithful service heretofore rendered to me and my family." By law, Bill was then required to secure permission from the county court in order to remain legally in Montgomery County. He could probably have ignored this requirement. Many of the county's free people of color violated this requirement and never faced any legal consequences for their actions.

William Moon played it safe, though, perhaps because his wife and children remained enslaved, and he did not want to jeopardize his chances to
stay near them.[22]

Jacob Price's debt to William Ballard Preston clearly shows that the
men knew one another, and early in the 1820s, it seems, Price and Preston's father, James Patton Preston, had arranged for or permitted Moon to
marry Louisa, a woman enslaved at Smithfield. William probably continued to live and work with Price but was allowed to visit Louisa, who lived
at Smithfield with the couple's children. Between 1823 and 1837, William
and Louisa Moon had at least four children—Hiram, Preston, Saunders,
and Francis—all of whom became the property of James Patton Preston
through his ownership of their mother. After gaining his freedom, William
Moon initially went to work for another neighbor, Henry Linkous, but in
1841 he began working and probably living at Smithfield. In the meantime,
he had registered with county officials and had formally requested permission to remain in Montgomery County. Early in 1840 the county court
considered his request and declared: "it appearing to the court upon satisfactory proof made to them that the applicant is a person of good character,
peaceable, orderly and industrious, and not addicted to drunkenness, gam-
ing, or any other vice, the court doth grant him permission to remain within
the commonwealth and to reside within this county." But about this time
Louisa seems to have died or been sold. Thus, when James Patton Preston
died in 1843, the inventory of his estate included the Moons' four sons but
neither of their parents.[23]

The presence of families among the people enslaved at Smithfield in 1843
does not mean these families were always intact. Marsha and Frank Sanders, Eliza and Rubin Burke, and Richard and Margaret Saunders seem to
have lived apart, as did William and Louisa Moon, for much of their married lives. Nor did the other families enslaved at Smithfield remain intact
after the death of James Patton Preston. Four years later, in 1847, Preston's
slaves were divided among his four surviving children, and most of the
identifiable families at Smithfield were broken up. William and Catherine McNorton remained at Smithfield with William Ballard Preston. With
them were their eldest daughter, Marsha, and her son Harrison; a younger
daughter, Nancy; and the couple's two youngest sons, Orville and Robert,
who were six and five, respectively, when the division took place. At least
three of the McNortons' other children (and their granddaughter, Charlotte

Burke) went to James F. Preston at White Thorn, at least two went to Robert Preston at Solitude, and at least two went to Pittsylvania County with Catharine Preston Gilmer. A similar fate befell the Fraction family. John and Easther, their daughter Chloe (age twenty-one), and their three youngest sons—Oscar (age thirteen), Tom (age eight), and Wilson (age six)—became the property of Robert Preston at Solitude. Four of the Fractions' other children—Mary (age twenty-six), George (age twenty-four), Juda (age twenty), and Rebecca (age eleven)—remained at Smithfield, while Virginia (age eighteen) went to White Thorn, and Ellen (age fourteen) moved to Pittsylvania County. Margaret Saunders and at least three of her children—Edmonia, Charles, and Amanda—moved to White Thorn, while seventeen-year old Flora stayed at Smithfield, and Robert (age sixteen), Amy, (age fourteen), and David (age six), went to Solitude. The Moon brothers may also have been separated. The three youngest—Francis (age ten), Saunders (age fourteen), and Preston (age seventeen)—moved to the Gilmer plantation in Pittsylvania County, though it remains unclear where the eldest brother, Hiram (age twenty-three), went.[24]

Family members remaining at Smithfield, Solitude, and White Thorn after 1847 were probably able to maintain contact with one another with relatively little trouble. It is unclear how many quarters James Patton Preston had at Smithfield before his death, but the plantation was small enough that he may have had just one. If that was the case, even after the division of his estate some of the individuals whose ownership had passed to Robert or James F. Preston may have continued living with their kin at Smithfield for several years. Eventually, Robert Preston did have his own quarters at Solitude and James F. Preston did at White Thorn, but these were little more than a mile from the Smithfield quarters, so frequent visits among the three plantations would still have been possible. Family members taken to Pittsylvania County, however, found themselves some ninety miles from Montgomery County. For them, visits were certainly less frequent, if they ever occurred, and probably stopped entirely when Catharine Preston Gilmer died in early 1852. Emotional bonds, however, continued to tie many of the separated individuals to parents and siblings they left behind, and at least four of those taken to Pittsylvania County returned to Montgomery County when they gained their freedom in 1865.[25]

Family formation continued among the enslaved after the distribution of James Patton Preston's estate. When freedpeople in Virginia were permitted to register and legalize their marriages in 1866, those who did so in Montgomery County included nine couples in which one or both partners identified one of the Prestons as their former owner and had probably been living in Montgomery County before gaining their freedom. Four other couples identified George Gilmer (who had inherited the property of his deceased wife, Catharine Preston) as their former owner and had been living in Pittsylvania County until 1865. Only one of these thirteen couples, Margaret and Richard Saunders, had been together in 1843; the others had all married between 1850 and 1864. Like the couples found on the inventory of James Patton Preston's estate, those included on the cohabitation register had lived in a variety of circumstances before their emancipation, but at least six and perhaps as many as ten of the thirteen had been living together as resident couples.[26]

The four freedpeople known to have moved back from Pittsylvania County after slavery ended had each married another person enslaved by George Gilmer and had apparently lived with their spouses and children on his plantation until 1865. Among those who had remained in Montgomery County, at least two enslaved couples seem to have lived together after marriage. In 1866, Thomas Banks and Maria Lewis both named William Ballard Preston as their last owner, while Taylor McNorton and Syrena Montague both named Sarah Preston, the widow of James F. Preston, as theirs. At least three other individuals on the cohabitation register with links to Smithfield seem to have been in abroad marriages. Margaret Dandridge had been in such a marriage with Richard Saunders since 1825. More recently, Charlotte Burke, who lived at White Thorn, had married John Smith, who had been enslaved by Henry Burnet in Henry County, and Henry Johnson, enslaved at Smithfield, had married Louisa Bone, who identified her last owner as a Preston Pugh of Montgomery County.[27]

Four other couples included on the Montgomery County cohabitation register reported that the partners had had different owners but still may have lived together because in each of these cases the different owners were two Prestons who owned adjoining plantations. John Fraction, who lived at Solitude, remarried after the death of Easther, and his new wife, Fanny Johnson, lived at Smithfield. Fraction's son, Othello, also lived at Solitude and also married a woman, Mary Carr, who probably lived at Smithfield. Orville McNorton, at Smithfield, married Easter Jane Fraction, who lived at White Thorn, and Elizabeth Burks, at White Thorn, married William

Poindexter, who probably lived at Smithfield. At least two of these couples, John and Fanny Fraction and Orville and Easter Jane McNorton, certainly lived on or adjacent to Smithfield. The other two couples, Othello and Mary Fraction and Elizabeth and William Poindexter, probably did, though Mary Fraction and William Poindexter may have lived in Henry County, where William Ballard Preston owned three plantations and at least 150 enslaved workers.[28]

Looking at all of the marriages known or likely among those enslaved by the Prestons suggests that marriage was common but far from universal among the men and women held at Smithfield during the nineteenth century. The inventory of James Patton Preston's estate names thirty-nine enslaved individuals aged sixteen or older. Among those thirty-nine, fourteen were women with children or individuals known to have been married, so it seems that at least a third of the adults enslaved at Smithfield in 1843 were involved in relationships of some kind. The age at which they entered those relationships is also difficult to gauge precisely. For men, the median age was 17 on the inventory and 23.5 on the cohabitation register, while for women the ages were 19 and 21.5, but both the inventory and the cohabitation register present challenges to estimating the age at which enslaved men and women first married. It is clear, however, that at least some of those married at Smithfield remained together for many years. The cohabitation register includes thirteen marriages involving freedpeople with a connection Smithfield. The median duration of these unions was only three years in 1866, but they included marriages that had endured ten, sixteen, and forty-one years. In addition, John Fraction's first marriage had lasted more than thirty years before Easther's death, and William and Catherine McNorton, both of whom died before the cohabitation register was compiled, were together for more than thirty years.[29]

Ultimately, the men and women enslaved at Smithfield had little control over whether or not to enter long-term relationships or with whom to enter them. The relationships they did form had no legal standing and could be ended at any time by the owner of either partner in the relationship. And enslaved parents had little control over the lives of their children. Despite this brutal reality, individuals enslaved at Smithfield were often able to form families and to maintain them over generations. This may have been, in part at least, because the Prestons sometimes decided that the best way to promote their own interests was to allow those they enslaved some hope of enjoying family lives. However, it may also have been a lucky result of demographics and economics; for much of its history, the enslaved population of Smithfield was large enough to provide marriage partners for many of its members but not so large that the Prestons routinely felt the need to sell "excess" hands to the expanding Cotton South. Whether by luck or design, many of those enslaved at Smithfield during the nineteenth century were able to establish families, and it seems clear that family was important to them. The connections they maintained after gaining their freedom, and the frequency with which they named their children after siblings, parents, and other members of the family suggest very strong bonds of attachment. As it was for others enslaved elsewhere in the South, family was a key element in the struggle for survival for the men and women at Smithfield. It was source of emotional and material support, a public sign of their humanity, and a refuge from the brutality of the system in which they found themselves trapped.

3

Life and Work in the Quarters

Physically, the center of slave life on any southern plantation was the quarters. This might be a cluster of small cabins or an avenue of orderly brick cottages, but whatever their precise shape or appearance, the quarters were home to most of those enslaved on a particular plantation. The quarters provided more than housing, though. They were generally far enough from the main house or the overseer's quarters to provide enslaved workers a temporary escape from the constant supervision that was part of slavery. In the quarters they could talk honestly to one another, could mourn their losses together, and could celebrate their victories in the constant battle of wits between themselves and their masters and overseers. In a world where nearly all of life's most important decisions were outside of their control, the quarters offered a small space in which the enslaved had at least some power over their own lives.

Most of those enslaved at Smithfield lived in distinct quarters established on one of the Preston plantations. Some of those with domestic responsibilities—cooks, nurses, and house servants—may have lived in the main house or in nearby dependencies, such as an outside kitchen, but most probably lived in the quarters. By 1860, separate quarters existed at Smithfield, Solitude, and White Thorn. Census-takers that year were instructed to count "what number of separate tenements are occupied by slaves," and the enumerator in Montgomery County reported eight "slave houses" at Smithfield, ten at Solitude, and six at White Thorn. Unfortunately, it is impossible to say when any of these were built. They may all date to the early years before Smithfield was divided, or they may have been established at different times as the estate was divided, and separate plantations were established at Solitude and White Thorn. Whatever their origins, the number of houses in the quarters no doubt grew over time as the enslaved population grew.

Unfortunately, the quarters at Smithfield have not survived nor have archaeologists located their remains, but clues have survived indicating their location and their nature. They were probably located several hundred yards southeast of the main house. Preston family tradition says the quarters were along the plantation's main drive, which originally entered from the east and then turned north to approach the south-facing doorway of the main house, and according to the 1865 deed that divided Smithfield among the heirs of William Ballard Preston, three "cabins," a "double cabin," and "the overseer's house" stood in this vicinity.[1] This is also the site of a centuries-old white oak tree that probably stood at the heart of the quarters at Smithfield. Known as the Merry Oak, it stood until a storm shattered its trunk in May of 2020, and descendants of both the Prestons and the families they enslaved have identified the tree as a place where those enslaved at Smithfield met to mark special events. This was almost certainly an echo of traditions carried aboard the *True Blue* from West Africa and brought to southwest Virginia by those first sixteen captives purchased by William Preston. Sacred trees have long played important roles in the religions and cultures of West Africa. Among the Gurensi people of northern Ghana, for example, sacred trees are seen as the dwelling places of powerful ancestors, the providers of protection to the descendants of those ancestors, mediums through which to communicate with God, and promoters of unity and solidarity in the community. Such trees often stand near the centers of West African villages, and the Merry Oak seems to have stood at or near the center of the quarters at Smithfield.[2]

The houses around the Merry Oak were probably simple log structures. The deed partitioning Smithfield distinguished between a number of cabins, which had probably housed the enslaved, and the overseer's house, which may have been a frame structure. At White Thorn, log outbuildings that may have housed enslaved families stood near the main house until they were taken down during the twentieth century. Photographs of the buildings (including one later moved to Smithfield) show they were clearly log that had been covered in sawn timber at some point. A similar structure in which enslaved domestic servants probably lived has survived just east

The Merry Oak, which stood near the likely site of the quarters at Smithfield. (Author's collection; photograph by Kerri Moseley-Hobbs)

of the main house at Solitude. Perhaps the best indication of what slave housing at Smithfield might have looked like, though, comes from a structure that, until it was moved recently, stood at Greenfield: William Preston's original plantation home.[3]

After Preston's death, Greenfield passed to his son John and then to John's daughter Susanna and her husband, William Radford. During the Radfords' tenure, the owners built or had built a double cabin that historians believe was intended to house some of the plantation's enslaved workers. Standing two hundred feet from the main house, the building consisted of two one-story log pens, each about sixteen-by-eighteen feet. The pens

Housing for those enslaved at Smithfield probably resembled this double cabin built for enslaved workers at Greenfield. (Virginia Department of Historic Resources)

were covered by a single roof, and between them stood a central limestone and brick chimney with fireboxes facing into the living area on each side. Each of the two units had a separate entrance and, on the ground floor, a single window in the wall opposite the door. Their interiors had wooden floors resting on log joists and walls that seem to have been whitewashed log with no trim or decorative woodwork. A ladder in each provided access to the loft space, which was unheated and lit by a window in the gable of the end wall opposite the chimney. It is impossible to be certain, but this may closely resemble the "double cabin" mentioned at Smithfield in 1865.[4]

The quarters may also have contained small gardens in which families enslaved by the Prestons raised vegetables on their own time and for their own use. No definitive evidence of gardens has survived at Smithfield, Solitude, or White Thorn, but they were a common feature on southern plantations, and their presence at Smithfield would hardly be surprising. Gardens offered multiple benefits to enslaved men and women. Obviously, they provided an additional source of food to supplement their rations, but the psychological benefit of gardens was just as important. They allowed enslaved people to exercise autonomy in at least one aspect of their lives and schedules. Enslaved families could raise what *they* chose to plant and dispose of the harvest as *they* saw fit. Gardens even enabled some enslaved workers to make money for themselves. Legally, slaves had no property rights, and anything they grew belonged to their owners. Many slave owners, however, permitted workers who raised vegetables or chickens on their own time to sell or trade what they produced and keep for themselves whatever cash or goods they received in return. Some plantation owners objected to gardens on the grounds that they diverted workers' energy away from the owners' crops or that they provided cover for theft of the owners' produce, but they remained a common feature on antebellum plantations, and it seems likely that they existed at Smithfield, Solitude, and White Thorn.[5]

In general, living conditions in the quarters at Smithfield seem to have been simple but adequate. The only surviving material evidence of the lives of the enslaved is from an outbuilding at Solitude in which some of Robert Preston's domestic workers lived between 1840 and 1865. Here, archaeologists concluded: "the vast majority of the artifacts that appear to date to the antebellum occupation are utilitarian in nature. Little was found to suggest the presence of expendable income. Artifacts associated with the consumption of tobacco, for example, are notably absent. Personal items were rarely encountered. The clothing items consisted of basic, unstylized buttons and buckles. The peculiar lack of artifacts relating to leisure activities again suggests impoverished conditions as well as, one could argue, the strictly limited freedom that slaves endured." Documentary evidence from the estate of William Ballard Preston also suggests that enslaved workers at Smithfield enjoyed a simple lifestyle. After Preston's death, the owners of a woolen mill in Rappahannock County presented a claim against the estate for "winter clothing for servants" and indicated that Preston had been a customer of theirs "for several years previous to the war." Court records in Montgomery County sometimes mention that slaves there received "the customary suits of summer and winter clothing shoes socks hat and blanket," and the specific reference to "winter clothing" suggests that Preston, too, provided his workers summer and winter clothing, and that the latter was wool.[6]

The fact that people enslaved at Smithfield enjoyed adequate housing and clothing was certainly not a sign of the Prestons' concern for them *as people*, though. From the Prestons' perspective, it simply made good economic sense to provide a level of care for their workers that ensured they remained healthy enough to work for as many years as possible. This also explains the Prestons' willingness to provide medical care to their enslaved workers comparable to that the family itself received. It is impossible to say when this began, but in 1850 William Ballard Preston contracted with Dr. Harvey Black, a young Blacksburg physician, to provide medical care for his enslaved workforce. Black continued to care for all the residents of Smithfield—enslaved and free—until the spring of 1861, when the doctor left to serve in the Confederate army. Preston then turned to Dr. James Otey for a year and then to Dr. Henry Ribble, who continued providing medical services through the end of the Civil War. James F. Preston and Robert T. Preston also employed Dr. Black from 1855 to 1861, though it is impossible to say if they did so before 1855 or if they made use of Drs. Otey or Ribble after Harvey Black entered the army.[7]

The doctors' accounts record almost daily visits, including frequent night visits, to Smithfield, Solitude, and White Thorn. Some of these calls were to care for members of the Preston family, but the great majority were to see enslaved individuals, who were usually identified by name in the record. The most common entry is simply "visit pres med," but the accounts also identify a number of specific remedies and procedures. Among the remedies provided were cod liver oil, castor oil, laudanum, and a host of herbal and patent medicines such as pink root (a dewormer), blue mass (a mercury-based medicine then widely used for a variety of ailments), and Husband's Calcined Magnesia (advertised as "highly beneficial in all diseases of the stomach and bowels which are attended with acidity"). The most common procedures identified in the accounts were pulling teeth, bleeding, and blistering, though the doctors occasionally set broken bones or provided treatment for syphilis. Obstetrical procedures—delivery of a child or of the afterbirth—are rare in the doctors' accounts. In the early nineteenth century childbirth was generally the responsibility of midwives rather than doctors, and enslaved women almost certainly served as midwives in the Prestons' quarters.[8]

Family and quarters were the most important forms of community among the enslaved at Smithfield, but they were not the only ones. Religion also brought them together, and like family, religion crossed property lines and brought together people from a number of different plantations. Independent Black churches were illegal in Virginia until after the Civil War.

Black congregations could meet legally if they were under White supervision, but there is no evidence that this happened anywhere in Montgomery County. Instead, many of those enslaved in the county—including a number of those at Smithfield—joined their owners in churches with biracial congregations under White control. In Montgomery County, at least nine congregations in three different denominations included enslaved men or women among their members. The largest number were Methodists, which was also the largest White denomination in the county and had included Black members since 1844, at least. By the early 1860s, 125 enslaved adults belonged to Methodist congregations in the county, and they made up more than a third of Methodist church membership in the county. Montgomery County's Presbyterian churches also included enslaved members. They were fewer in number than the Methodists, however, and made up only about three percent of the county's Presbyterian faithful. Finally, there was also a handful of Black Baptists in Montgomery County: four among eighty-three Baptists in the county in 1860.[9]

At Smithfield, Methodism reigned supreme. The Preston family had originally been Presbyterian but converted to Methodism sometime after settling in Virginia. Their enslaved workers then followed—or were required to follow—the family's lead. White Southerners, including Methodists, had long seen religion as a useful tool in justifying and maintaining the institution of slavery and used it to serve their own interests by emphasizing those parts of the Gospel that called on servants to remain obedient. Methodists had operated a separate "plantation mission" since 1829 that targeted slaves in the southern United States. Church leaders adapted a catechism originally written for children, modified it "to inculcate the duties of servants to their masters," and presented to slaves what one history of the church has called "a strange Methodism of law and obedience, not grace and love."[10] Methodist leaders encouraged masters to bring their workers to church, and one can imagine a small procession riding and marching from Smithfield, Solitude, and White Thorn into Blacksburg to attend services. It is impossible to say how many of the Prestons' enslaved workers attended services with them, but at least nine became full members of the church while still enslaved. William McNorton, Catherine McNorton, Easter Jane McNorton, Elizabeth Poindexter, Virginia Caperton, Amanda Saunders, Edward Saunders, Thomas Banks, and Maria Lewis all appear on a list of "colored members" compiled sometime in the early 1860s. Several other men and women who had been enslaved by the Prestons until 1865 appear on an 1866 membership list, though it is impossible to say if they joined before or after their emancipation. On arriving, however, White and Black members moved to separate sections of the church on the basis of their race: Whites sat on the ground floor, while Blacks were relegated to the gallery.[11]

It remains unclear exactly what church membership meant in the case of an enslaved Methodist, but to a limited degree it may have provided them an enhanced sense of self-esteem. Church records are almost the only records from antebellum Montgomery County in which enslaved individuals were regularly identified by their full names. Whites generally referred to enslaved Blacks by their first names only, though they sometimes added a modifier such as "Old" or "Aunt." They rarely employed a surname, even when it is clear that enslaved people had surnames and that owners often knew them. Court records, manumission documents, and private accounts occasionally identify enslaved individuals by their full names, as do a few records from the Presbyterian Church, but only the Methodists routinely accorded enslaved members this level of dignity. Lists of Black members in Blacksburg invariably identify individuals by their full names, with surnames that were rarely the same as their masters'. In a further sign of respect, Methodist church records regularly identified enslaved women who were married by their married names. This was a small but significant acknowledgment that, in one regard at least, Black Methodists were equal to their White co-religionists.[12]

Church membership also provided enslaved men and women an opportunity to meet openly with one another in a group of their own. Methodist congregations were usually divided into "classes" whose members met separately to study and worship in smaller groups, and separate Black classes appeared in Montgomery County as early as 1844. Black classes in the Blacksburg church had White leaders, but class meetings still represented a rare opportunity for Black members to come together and demonstrate their commitment to the church and their understanding of its tenets. It also provided them an opportunity, like their owners, to show their commitment to the Lord through financial contributions. Methodist quarterly meetings regularly include cash contributions from a "Colored" collection or from a "Black Class" in Blacksburg.[13]

Any suggestion of equality between Black and White Methodists, however, was still quite limited. Black baptisms, for example, were rare in the county. The only baptisms performed for enslaved Methodists were twelve performed in Blacksburg on a single day in 1863. Church records from the era are entirely silent regarding enslaved members and communion. It seems inconceivable that enslaved members would not be offered this sacrament of the church, but it is equally inconceivable that Blacks and Whites would have received it together. Elsewhere in the South, Blacks took communion after Whites did or in separate services, and this was undoubtedly the case in Montgomery County, too. Marriages among enslaved church members were also problematic. Methodists in the county often recorded White marriages in their church registers; marriages by enslaved couples, however, were never recorded, although married women were identified by their married names rather than their birth names. Like most White Southerners, Methodists continued to believe that slave owners were free to separate enslaved couples, and it appears that the congregation was discouraged from considering unions between the enslaved as on par with those of White communicants.[14]

Religion at Smithfield was probably not confined to the peculiar form offered by the Methodist church in Blacksburg. The people enslaved at Smithfield almost certainly worshipped by themselves as well. Though it was illegal in Virginia for Blacks to preach without White supervision or even to learn to read the Bible on their own, small numbers of Black Virginians did learn to read and smaller numbers felt called to preach. They were central figures in a widespread network of covert churches that are best known from the narratives of ex-slaves collected during the 1930s. Some met in the quarters or in barns if they were sufficiently distant from prying White eyes. Many also met in "brush arbors." These were often simply clearings in the forest to which enslaved people returned for clandestine services, but enslaved worshippers did sometimes build temporary structures of logs or branches in woodlands adjacent to the quarters. "We jes made er bush arbor by cuttin' bushes dat was full of green leaves an' puttin' 'em on top of four poles reachin' from pole to pole," recalled Arthur Greene of the practice in Nottoway County. Services were led by one of their own and combined elements that reflected White religious practices, such as hymns and sermons, with those, such as shouts, rooted in African spiritual practices. Minnie Folkes, for example, said of the services she remembered in Chesterfield County, "mettin's was carried on jes' like we do today somewhatly. . . . Only diffe'nce is de slaves dat knowed de mos' bout de Bible would tell an' explain what God told him a vision . . . an' den dey prayed for dis vision to come to pass."[15]

Few narratives have survived from anyone enslaved in Montgomery County, and none of those that have survived describe brush arbors or secret Black gatherings. Extant records do, however, show that enslaved workers organized religious activity in the county, including the area around Smithfield. It also shows that while such activity was technically illegal it was tolerated by White officials. The best-known Black preacher in Montgomery County was Richard Taylor. He was enslaved by George Earhart, who lived east of Blacksburg and was a member of Trinity Church, a smaller congregation that together with the Blacksburg congregation made up the Methodists' Blacksburg Station. Taylor was also a lay preacher who led services and performed weddings in the region around Blacksburg for several decades before slavery ended in the county. According to an obituary published in 1879, Taylor "became a preacher of the gospel about fifty years ago, and was permitted by his master to preach whereever he felt called to go, and was listened to with profit by white and black alike," and at least one woman who had been enslaved in the county recalled Taylor officiating at her wedding in about 1850. No evidence has survived that Richard Taylor ever preached at Smithfield or performed a wedding there, but his proximity and his connection through the Blacksburg Station certainly make it possible that he did.[16]

Family, church, and celebrations in the quarters were sources of refuge for the people enslaved at Smithfield. Most of their time, though, was given over to work. At its heart, slavery was a system designed to provide labor for the benefit of a worker's owner, and that was certainly true at Smithfield. The Preston family managed thousands of acres of farmland and a variety of business operations, all of which depended on enslaved labor. In addition, the Prestons lived in homes built and maintained by enslaved workers and relied on them to prepare their food, to wash their clothes, to care for their children, and to provide a host of other domestic services.

Agriculture was the foundation of the Prestons' wealth, which was built on grain and livestock rather than tobacco, an important cash crop for many Virginia plantations. The Prestons certainly understood tobacco cultivation. Through his marriage to Lucy Redd, William Ballad Preston acquired three plantations in Henry County on which enslaved workers produced thousands of pounds of tobacco each year. And it was certainly possible to raise tobacco at Smithfield. Until the 1850s, though, it made little economic sense to do so because it was so difficult to get the crop to market. Montgomery County lay so far upstream that the Roanoke River was too shallow for commercial traffic, and the New River, while useful for local trade, was interrupted by rapids and falls farther downstream that blocked access from southwest Virginia to the rest of the Ohio/Mississippi system. Farmers in the county did enjoy good road connections to markets farther east via the South West Turnpike, which had an engineered, all-weather surface and was one of the best roads in the region. Still, the expense of land transportation made it difficult to move bulky products such as tobacco profitably from Montgomery County to distant markets. Not until the arrival of the Virginia and Tennessee Railroad, in 1854, did commercial tobacco farming take off in Montgomery County.[17]

By then, however, the Prestons had established profitable plantations based on grain and livestock. William Preston had established Smithfield growing hemp, but demand for Virginia hemp fell sharply after Preston's death; poor quality Virginia hemp simply could not compete with higher quality hemp produced in Kentucky or imported from Russia.[18] As the market for hemp evaporated, Preston's heirs turned to a mix of products they could market profitably. The most important of these was wheat. Because so many other farmers in the county also raised wheat, local demand for Smithfield's harvest was limited. Wheat could be shipped to market though, or more profitably, could be processed locally and exported as flour. To tap this market, the Prestons raised thousands of bushels of wheat each year and by 1816 had built a gristmill at Smithfield. This enabled the family to turn its own wheat into flour and to collect a share of the flour produced from any neighbor's wheat processed at the mill. Livestock was a key source of income for the Prestons. Cattle provided meat and milk, both of which could be profitably transported to market: animals destined for slaughter could be driven to market, while milk could be transported safely in the form of butter. Sheep could also be driven to market but were probably more important for the wool they provided. Finally, Smithfield also produced a variety of crops mainly for home consumption, including large quantities of corn, oats, potatoes, and hay. The Prestons also raised hundreds of pigs. Some of this bounty may have been sold locally or sent to more distant markets, but much of it was probably consumed on the plantation.[19]

At Smithfield, of course, it was enslaved workers who actually raised the cattle, as well as wheat, corn, and other crops, and most of the men enslaved there probably worked as farm laborers. No census or inventory from Smithfield describes the occupations of workers enslaved there, but that was one of the questions on the cohabitation register. The register only includes seven men who had been enslaved at Smithfield, White Thorn, or Solitude, but six of the seven identified themselves as "farmer." While this probably represents less than a quarter of the working-age men on the Prestons' plantations in Montgomery County, it does suggest the overwhelming extent to which enslaved men on those plantations performed agricultural labor.[20] And the variety of crops raised at Smithfield meant that farmworkers there performed a variety of tasks. Wheat, corn, potatoes, and hay all had different planting and harvesting schedules, and workers rotated among the crops over the course of the season. There was also the labor associated with raising and caring for livestock, shearing sheep, and slaughtering hogs as well as with the construction and maintenance of barns, fences, and the rest of the agricultural infrastructure. This may have spared the Prestons' workers the repetitive nature of work on a plantation dominated by tobacco, but it may also have meant they worked more during the year as they moved back and forth among the different crops and tasks.[21]

Much of this work was performed under the eyes of an overseer. Like many other owners of large plantations, especially those active in politics or the military, the Prestons often employed overseers to supervise their enslaved workers and manage their estates' daily operations. William Ballard Preston certainly did so at Smithfield, and James F. Preston did so at White Thorn. Robert T. Preston, at Solitude, had a Black "head man"—an enslaved man appointed to oversee his fellow workers—but seems not to have hired an overseer. Unfortunately, little is known of how any of these men carried out their duties. Some of their peers in Montgomery County certainly made liberal use of the whip. Janie Milton recalled her grandmother's description of work she performed while enslaved on another farm in the county: "[T]here was a man walking behind her with a black-snake whip and 'wham' he'd hit her right around her waist. She'd be ho'in corn. If she slacked just a little bit, they swatted out, 'wham.'" What happened on the Prestons' plantations, however, remains a mystery. Surviving letters from William Ballard Preston to his overseers focus on larger issues, such as how much and what to plant, or on general directives to maintain good order. He said nothing specific about how to do that.[22]

Enslaved men may also have worked as craftsmen at Smithfield, though it is impossible to identify with certainty most of those who did so. Family tradition among the Prestons' descendants maintains that several pieces of furniture now on display at Smithfield or Solitude were built by enslaved artisans, but none of those artisans' names have come down to us. Walter McNorton, who was born at Smithfield, trained as a carpenter but probably not until after he moved to Pittsylvania County following the division of James Patton Preston's estate. Similarly, William Poindexter identified himself as a blacksmith on the cohabitation register and named William Ballard Preston as his last owner, but Poindexter was born in Henry County and as a slave may have worked on one of Preston's plantations in that county rather than at Smithfield.

Enslaved women also performed important roles in Smithfield's agricultural economy. Milking cows and churning the milk into butter was generally "women's work" on antebellum farms and plantations as was tending kitchen gardens and raising chickens. Enslaved women may also have worked in the fields alongside men, though. This was certainly common elsewhere in the plantation South, and Janie Milton, whose grandmother had been enslaved on another farm in Montgomery County, recalled a woman on the farm, Ruby Henderson, who had worked in the fields: "she was the lead worker in the yard doin everything but cradlin the grain: choppin' the corn, bindin' the sheaths. A man would be cradlin' and he'd throw it and she'd catch it right in her arms, and bind it, throw it over her shoulder, ready for the mixer."[23]

Both men and women also worked in the Preston households as cooks, nurses, and house servants. Virginia Fraction, who was born at Smithfield, moved to White Thorn as a young woman when the slaves of James Patton Preston were distributed among his children, and remained there until her death in 1891. After 1865 she was often identified as the family's cook, which suggests that she probably began cooking for the Prestons while she was still enslaved. Her daughter, Easter Jane Fraction McNorton, also seems to have been a house servant. In 1861, Mary Eliza Caperton, who was visiting her sister Sarah Ann at White Thorn, described waking up during a thunder storm and thinking that she felt rain blowing in through an open window. "I told Easter to get up & see the windows," she wrote, suggesting that Easter slept in the same room, as one might expect of a house servant. Easter's brother-in-law, Ballard McNorton, also worked as a house servant at White Thorn. He too was born at Smithfield and moved to White Thorn after the death of James Patton Preston. He may have performed other duties during his years there, but he was a house servant when he died in 1861. James F. Patton wrote that Ballard's death "leaves Mrs. Preston in great want of a house servant" and immediately began looking for "a reliable man which can be managed by a lady." [24]

Domestic servants were not confined to housework, though; they also accompanied family members who travelled on business, went to school, or joined the military. Daughters of William Ballard Preston, for example, took enslaved servants with them when they travelled to Richmond, and Preston men took them as cooks or servants when they joined the army. William Preston, son of the colonel, wanted to take an enslaved man with him when he was with the army on the Ohio frontier during the 1790s, but his mother objected on the grounds that "he may be set at liberty by the laws of the NW territory." It is unclear whether or not William ever did take a servant into the army with him, but James F. Preston did on two occasions. In 1846, Preston raised a company in what became the First Regiment of Virginia Volunteers for service in the Mexican War and took Taylor McNorton with him to cook for the officers' mess of his company. When the regiment reached Fortress Monroe to board ships bound for Mexico, McNorton was told that he could not travel with the troops "on account of his being a slave." Preston, however, prevailed upon the enrolling officer, and McNorton was allowed to accompany the regiment. He then spent a year in northern Mexico with Preston's company before returning to Virginia in July 1848. Thirteen years later, in 1861, Preston again took Taylor McNorton as "my servant man" when he joined the Confederate army. McNorton served Preston in that capacity until Preston died, early in 1862, and then cooked for Harvey Black, the doctor, who had also joined the army in 1861.[25]

Workers from Smithfield were also leased to other employers. Hiring enslaved workers was a common practice in the antebellum South because it provided distinct advantages to both the employer and the owner of the workers. Some of those hiring enslaved workers did so because they did not have the capital or credit necessary to buy them or did not need them long enough to justify their purchase price. Others preferred hiring because the nature of the work they wanted done was irregular and they wanted the greater flexibility that came with hiring, or the work was dangerous, and they preferred to risk other peoples' property instead of their own. For the owners of enslaved individuals, on the other hand, hiring them out provided additional income for those who had more hands than they needed at a given time and spared them the cost of supporting such surplus workers. Hiring also provided a means of profiting from enslaved workers while their ownership was in dispute, while estates were in probate, or when their owners were minors and unable to employ their labor themselves. In such cases, rental payments could be held by the court until the estate was settled or the dispute resolved or could be made to the minor owner's guardian to meet the expense of his or her care.[26]

It is impossible to say if all of the Prestons leased slaves, but William Ballard Preston certainly did. Between 1850 and 1865, he or his estate rented enslaved men to a variety of employers. Orville McNorton, then in his early twenties, was rented to a Beverly Johnston for the years 1862 and 1863, and in April of 1863 an unknown number of workers were rented for an unspecified period of time to the Confederate government. In these cases, it is impossible to say what sort of work the enslaved workers performed. In at least two cases, however, Preston leased workers to specific industrial operations. In 1851–52, for example, he rented at least one and perhaps as many as five men to John Buford, a contractor building the Virginia and Tennessee Railroad in Montgomery County. Antebellum railroad work was hard and dangerous, and Southern railroads frequently hired slaves to do it. Buford relied on twelve to fifteen enslaved men, along with free Black workers and Irish immigrants to build the section of the Virginia and Tennessee Railroad that crossed Montgomery County. These men cleared the right of way, dug and blasted a number of tunnels—work that Buford's partner called "a slow, tedious, laborious business," prepared the roadbed, and laid the track. Enslaved workers rarely performed the more skilled labor of blasting or of building stone viaducts for the railroad, nor do they seem to have been the ones laying down the rails. Instead, they generally filled, loaded, drove, and dumped carts of dirt and rock. Once construction was finished, in 1856, the railroad continued leasing enslaved men in the county to maintain and operate the line, though it is impossible to say if it hired any of Preston's men for this work.[27]

William Ballard Preston's estate also leased a number of enslaved men to an ironworks. Until the last quarter of the nineteenth century, most of the iron in the United States was produced by hundreds of small furnaces using relatively primitive technology to make simple cast-iron goods or pig iron—ingots of raw iron that went into the manufacture of more finished ironware and the bar stock used by blacksmiths. Making iron required iron ore, limestone, charcoal, and water, and ironworks were generally located where these raw materials were readily available. Southwest Virginia had all four, and a number of ironworks operated near Smithfield, including the Cloverdale and Catawba furnaces in Botetourt County and the Cedar Run Furnace in Wythe County. The key structure at each was a large, pyramid-shaped furnace built of stone or brick. These were open at the top for filling and had vents at the bottom through which air was forced in by bellows as well as a hearth in which molten iron collected before it was drawn off for casting. First, the furnace was filled with charcoal that was burned to heat the structure itself. Then it was "charged"—filled with measured layers of iron ore, limestone (used as a flux to remove impurities), and charcoal—and the blast began. It continued night and day for weeks or months. Workers continually refilled the furnace from the top as burning charcoal melted the ore, converted the limestone and impurities in the ore into slag, and left molten iron to be drawn off the hearth into casting beds.[28]

Some of the tasks involved in ironmaking required skilled workers. Founders supervised the process and had to understand every element of iron production; keepers also needed to understand the entire process as they managed the blast at night or when the founder was away; fillers had to layer the correct quantities of ore, limestone, and charcoal into the furnace for the blast to continue efficiently; and guttermen had to draw off the molten iron at just the right time. But unskilled labor was also essential to ironmaking. Streams needed to be dammed and their waters diverted to power the bellows; tons of ore, limestone, and charcoal had to be hauled to the mouth of the furnace to feed the blast; and acres of forest had to be cut and burned in order to produce the charcoal. In the southern Appalachians, this was just the sort of labor that leased slaves could provide. Surviving records do not indicate how often the Prestons may have rented men to work at iron furnaces, but they certainly did in 1864. Nor is it clear how many men this involved. Based on the income they generated, though, it seems to have been at least two dozen adult men.[29]

In the end, it is impossible to say how "bad" life was for the people enslaved at Smithfield, but life as a slave was never "good." Enslaved men and women had no freedom and enjoyed little control over major aspects of their lives. They lived under a regime maintained by law and by force—a regime in which they were told when and how to work, if and who they could marry, and where and how they and their families would live. They lived knowing their families could be separated at any time and the members dispersed so widely that they might never see one another again. And they lived with the knowledge that no matter how hard they worked or how well they behaved, their condition would probably never change. Within that bleak and brutal world, though, it is possible to recognize degrees of misery. Some owners were less bad than others, and some slaves lived in better situations than others. For the men, women, and children enslaved by the Prestons, life seems to have been no worse than it was for most of their contemporaries.

Almost nothing is known about discipline or the work regimen at Smithfield. Housing, clothing, and food there seem to have been typical as was the frequency of sales and family separations. William Preston all but ensured that enslaved families would be separated by directing his widow to divide his enslaved workers among the couple's children. James F. Preston, on the other hand, wrote in his will that he wished to avoid selling any of his enslaved workers "unless it shall be deemed necessary by my executors or by my wife in consequence of unsubordination or other bad conduct or unless it should be necessary to make sale of them or some of them to pay my debts." He also indicted that if any were sold, "it is my wish that good homes should be provided for them in Virginia if possible." And as noted above, the Prestons did separate the enslaved families at Smithfield. Twice between 1780 and 1850 the death of an owner led to the division of almost every family on the plantation, and the first such division sent a number of individuals to distant counties or out of Virginia entirely. And the Prestons certainly recognized the pain this caused among the affected families. In 1820, William's son John sold an unknown number of individuals enslaved on another Preston property in Montgomery County "to the Missouri." His overseer wrote to Preston that the people who were sold "all seemed to be in good spirits and very little affected at parting, except Clara and Sabry on parting with Maria who appeared to be very much troubled as the[y] said they did not expect ever to see her again." Such separations were an inevitable part of chattel slavery. The Prestons simply accepted them, and the people they enslaved suffered the consequences.[30]

Nor is there much evidence that the Prestons opposed slavery or that they wished to see it ended at Smithfield. William Ballard Preston is sometimes described as an opponent of slavery, even as an abolitionist, but this is accurate only in a very narrow sense. Like many of his contemporaries, most famously, perhaps, Thomas Jefferson, Preston did sometimes express a generalized opposition to slavery and a desire to see it abolished in Virginia at some unspecified time in the future. In 1832, as a member of the

House of Delegates, he did support a proposal to enact gradual emancipation in Virginia in order to reduce the danger of slave rebellions in the commonwealth, but only if emancipation was linked to the removal of Black Virginians to Africa. Preston did declare during the debate that an enslaved man had "a natural right to regain his liberty," but he rejected absolutely the notion of abolishing slavery immediately or of incorporating freed Blacks into Virginia society. "All that I claim on this question," he said, "is, that when the public necessity demanding their emancipation is greater than the public necessity for their retention as slaves, that then it is in the power of this or any subsequent Legislature" to do so. Moreover, the Prestons made little effort to free anyone they enslaved. At his death in 1821, William Preston Jr. directed his heirs to free one man, Nassau, after five more years of service to Preston's widow, and James F. Preston gave his widow, Sarah, the option to emancipate Taylor McNorton if she felt that his service warranted it. Evidently, Sarah did not, and Nassau seems to have been the only person the Prestons ever freed voluntarily. Several other slave owners in Montgomery County emancipated dozens of individuals during the antebellum years, but not the Prestons.[31]

Unfortunately, it is nearly impossible to recapture what the people enslaved there thought of life at Smithfield. No evidence has yet come to light of any recollections—either written or oral—from the enslaved community at Smithfield. Their actions are slightly more revealing, but the message they send is mixed. Some did run away from the Prestons. Jim Barbour, a man purchased by William Preston Jr. in 1812, had a wife in Norfolk and tried to rejoin her in 1814. He was caught, sold to another planter, and eventually drowned during another escape attempt. Another man, Isaac, may have escaped in 1861. That spring, James Marrs, a free man of color living in Montgomery County, was arrested for showing his freedom papers to Isaac, who was enslaved by James F. Preston. Owners worried that seeing freedom papers would make it easier for slaves to forge them and facilitate their escape. Isaac may have been hoping to escape, and he may have succeeded because when Preston died, early in 1862, Isaac was not listed on the inventory of his estate. Even if Isaac did not escape, though, others did. As described more fully in the next chapter, at least four and perhaps five men escaped from the Prestons and joined the Union army during the Civil War.[32]

Obviously, most of the men and women enslaved at Smithfield never escaped. Indeed, most of them probably never tried to, but that does not mean they were happy with their lives. Escaping slavery was both danger-ous and difficult, and a successful escape would almost certainly involve leaving family behind forever. Thomas Jefferson wrote in the Declaration of Independence: "all experience hath shewn that mankind are more disposed to suffer, while evils are sufferable, than to right themselves by abolishing the forms to which they are accustomed." Most of the people enslaved at Smithfield were equally cautious. They made the best they could of a dread-ful situation rather than risk death or permanent separation from everyone they knew and loved.

4

War Comes to Smithfield

Eventually, the Civil War would have a profound effect on the institution of slavery at Smithfield and on the lives of the people enslaved there. Initially, however, its impact was relatively limited. The war did affect a number of enslaved individuals: men who were taken as servants by Confederate officers or conscripted as laborers by the Confederate government, men who escaped slavery and volunteered to serve in the Union army, and the family members these men left behind. And it did generate a new element of excitement in the quarters; people enslaved at Smithfield knew what the war was about and knew what its outcome meant to them. But the war had little immediate impact on the institution of slavery at Smithfield. The Prestons continued to buy, sell, and lease enslaved workers as they had for decades, and those they held in bondage continued to live and work much as they had before the war began.

By 1861, the long-simmering dispute over slavery was just as heated in Montgomery County as it was elsewhere in the United States. White residents of the county were not all as radical as their counterparts in other parts of Virginia or the South, but their concerns about slavery and "Southern Rights" were abundantly clear. During the recent presidential election, the county newspaper had filled its pages with reports of "abolitionist" conspiracies or slave "insurrections" across the South and warned that the election of Abraham Lincoln would lead to Republicans "destroying the slave property of the South, and making the slave equal in rights with the white." Once Lincoln had been elected, the paper declared bluntly that "the naked issue now for Virginia to decide, is, whether she will go North or South,"

and once the Commonwealth cast its lot with the Confederacy, the editors announced their determination "to engage in the defence of the State
against Lincoln's mercenary hordes from the North."[1]

The county's White residents, however, were not the only ones following national events and discussing what those events might mean to them.
Blacks in Montgomery County, including those enslaved by the Preston
family, were also talking about the election of Abraham Lincoln. Mary Eliza
Caperton, the sister-in-law of James F. Preston, was visiting White Thorn
during the spring of 1861, and early in May she wrote that a Black man
she called "Uncle Davy" had made a pro-Lincoln speech to "his brethren
in Blacksburg." According to Caperton, Davy had told his audience "that
Lincoln was a second Christ and that all that the white people said about
Lincoln was a lie from beginning to end." Davy's exact identity is unknown,
but according to Caperton he was married to a woman enslaved at White
Thorn and was the father of Robert T. Preston's "head man"—the enslaved
worker who supervised others at Solitude and a man in whom Preston had
the "greatest confidence." Given the many connections among the families
enslaved at Smithfield, Solitude, and White Thorn, it seems likely that all
of them knew what Davy was talking about and had probably been holding
discussions of their own in the quarters.[2]

They rarely did so publicly, though, because White residents of Montgomery County were clearly on edge during the winter and spring of
1861. The local paper often printed stories describing unrest among slaves
throughout the South "now that massa Lincoln was elected," and the tension rose even higher after the attack on Fort Sumter. Just days after the
Virginia Convention voted in favor of secession, White residents of the
county moved to organize a new mounted police force of one hundred
armed men for the purpose of patrolling the county and watching for any
dangerous activity by White Unionists, free people of color, or rebellious
slaves. At Smithfield, however, the Prestons seem to have believed their
workers were loyal, and that preserving their loyalty was simply a matter
of insulating them from dangerous outsiders. Early in May, William Ballard
Preston outlined this view in a letter to William Linkous, the overseer of his
Henry County plantations: "All over Virginia the Negroes are quiet & much
alarmed at the state of things. They are afraid & docile & obedient than ever
known and only want to be strictly managed, kept at home, and at work. I
am sure proper steps are taken in Henry for patroles & keep my Negroes

at home at all the places both day & night and keep others away." This faith was soon tested, however, when rumors swirled through the neighborhood of a plot to incite a rebellion among the county's enslaved population—including those on the Prestons' plantations.[3]

At the center of the alleged plot were two neighbors of the Prestons: Enos Price, a White man, and Washington, a Black man enslaved by Dr. James Otey. Witnesses claimed that Price met several times with Washington and urged him to take violent action. Price reportedly told Washington, "Lincoln would free the slaves but the only way he could do so would be to get rid of such men as the negros' master." He then directed Washington to visit a number of large plantations in the neighborhood, including Smithfield, Solitude, and White Thorn, and tell those enslaved there that "Saturday night was the night for their work." Price was arrested soon after meeting with Washington, and nothing came of his plot, but the Prestons remained nervous. Ten days after Price's arrest, Mary Eliza Caperton wrote from White Thorn that she had been awakened by a violent thunderstorm, "and the thought flashed across my mind that perhaps the Prices were about to attack us." She relaxed after realizing that it was not a slave rebellion, that lightening had struck the stable and set it on fire, but the reaction at Smithfield was far more dramatic: "The consternation at Smithfield they say was truly awful. The storm was not so bad there and they did not think of lightening. The servants gave the alarm and Mr. Preston jumped up, called for his pistol and knife and started off. In about 15 minutes after we were roused 4 of the home guard from Blacksburg came riding up with guns, but Mr. Legerwood [the overseer at White Thorn] told them they could put down their horses and guns and come help fight the fire."[4]

There is no evidence that anyone enslaved by the Prestons was actually involved in whatever Enos Price was planning, though, and life around Smithfield soon settled back into a fairly normal routine that proved remarkably immune to the disruption of war. Montgomery County was relatively distant from the war's major theatres. No large bodies of troops were stationed there, Union troops passed through the county just once before the final weeks of the war, and no large battles were ever fought there. Residents of the county did face shortages and inflation, but little of the massive upheaval that occurred in other parts of the South. As a result, life for many of those enslaved at Smithfield, Solitude, and White Thorn remained much the same during the war as it had been before.

The few surviving records of life at Smithfield during the war do not suggest that the Prestons or those they held in slavery experienced the shortages of food, clothing, and other daily necessities that some of their neighbors did. The family was still wealthy enough to travel, shop, and pay for the children's private education, and the plantation still produced abundant supplies of food. Indeed, food production at Smithfield probably increased during the war. In May 1861, William Ballard Preston directed the overseer of his Henry County plantations to plant more food: "I want you *at once* to put in at all the places *increased crops of corn* potatoes vegetables beans peas and everything that men require for food and try by all means to have a little to spare for *our country* and its defenders." No such order has survived from Smithfield, where Preston could speak directly to the overseer without having to write him a letter, but it seems likely that one was issued. Items the plantation did not produce itself, however, may have been unavailable or in short supply during the war. Before the war, for example, William Ballard Preston regularly bought winter clothing for his slaves from a woolens mill in Rappahannock County operated by J. G. and H. B. Miller, but the mill was destroyed early in the war. There is no evidence the Prestons ever found an alternative source of winter clothing, so those enslaved at Smithfield may have gone without.[5]

Wartime conditions also meant that those enslaved at Smithfield probably had to work harder during the war. On the one hand, the amount of work to be done on the plantation increased. The combination of military and civilian needs meant that demand for Smithfield's cattle, grain, and hay increased. If, as suggested above, Preston sought to meet this rising demand by increasing production on the plantation, he probably demanded longer hours from his enslaved workers. And growing more food and fodder was not the only demand on workers' time. Farm and household facilities still had to be maintained and repaired, and members of the Preston family still expected enslaved servants to handle their domestic needs. While the work to be done increased, however, the number of workers available to do it often declined. As described more fully below, state and Confederate officials pressed enslaved men from Smithfield into government service during the war, and members of the Preston family who joined the army sometimes took enslaved men with them to serve as cooks and servants.

Despite such disruptions, life went on for those enslaved by the Prestons. At least five marriages took place during the war in which one or both parties lived at Smithfield, Solitude, or White Thorn. William Poindexter and Elizabeth Burkes, Thomas Banks and Maria Lewis, Orville McNorton and Easter Jane Fraction, and Othello Fraction and Mary Carr were all enslaved by the Prestons. So too was Charlotte Burke, though her husband, John Smith, was not. And in keeping with a common practice, four of the five weddings took place at Christmas. Southern planters often allowed their enslaved workers to enjoy an extended holiday at Christmas. House servants, of course, were still expected to work, but field work was often curtailed so people could celebrate the holiday. This was also a popular time to celebrate weddings in the quarters. In Montgomery County, for example, the cohabitation register compiled in 1866 to legalize unions formed under slavery provides the dates on which 303 of those unions began. Thirty-three (10.9 percent) occurred on Christmas Day and a total of forty-seven (15.5 percent) during the last ten days of December. Among those enslaved by the Prestons, brides and grooms often came from large families with relatives at each of the family's plantations, so these weddings probably brought people together from Smithfield, Solitude, and White Thorn.[6]

Birth and death in the enslaved community also continued during the war years. Between 1861 and 1865, at least six children were born to women enslaved on the Prestons' Montgomery County plantations, and there may have been more because the reporting of slave births in the county was quite haphazard. All births and deaths in the county were supposed to be reported to county officials, but in practice relatively few owners of slaves reported either births or deaths to the proper authorities. The Prestons, in fact, reported no births to county officials during the war years, though post-emancipation records indicate that at least six children were born during those years to women enslaved by the family. And at least five individuals enslaved by the Prestons died during the war years. Two young men at Solitude, Wilson and Granville Fraction, drowned during the summer of 1862. Their deaths were reported to county officials but *how* they drowned was not. It may have been a work-related accident; they may have been fishing or swimming on their own time; or they may have been trying to cross the New River on their way to Ohio or Union-occupied territory in what later became West Virginia. In addition, Ballard McNorton, then in his early thirties, died at Solitude in 1861, while his parents, William and Catherine McNorton, died at Smithfield sometime between 1862 and 1864.[7]

The great mystery of the war years at Smithfield is what happened there in May 1864, when Union troops passed through Montgomery County and camped in Blacksburg. In an effort to destroy Confederate supplies and infrastructure, Union infantry under Brigadier General George Crook had marched south from West Virginia's Kanawha Valley to destroy saltworks, lead mines, and railroad facilities in southwest Virginia. After defeating Confederate forces at Cloyd's Mountain and destroying the railroad depot and several warehouses at Dublin, Crook's men then moved east along the rail line toward Montgomery County. There they destroyed a vital railroad bridge spanning the New River and additional facilities at Central Depot (modern Radford) before moving on to Blacksburg, where they spent a day resting and gathering supplies and camped overnight. One resident recalled that "they took everything they could to eat and destroyed the rest," while another reported that Union soldiers threatened to burn the homes of townspeople who refused to provide them with food. The troops' presence also provided a powerful symbol of freedom to the county's enslaved residents. Captain R. B. Wilson, whose Twelfth Ohio Infantry was part of Crook's force, wrote later that slaves "flocked to our ranks from every quarter" as Union troops made their way across the county. Dozens then followed Crook's forces as they returned to West Virginia. "Colored people . . . manifested the wildest joy at the advent of Massa Lincum's army," wrote Wilson, and "flocked to our army in such numbers that they threatened to become embarrassing to its progress."[8]

William Moon, a free Black man who had been married to a woman enslaved at Smithfield and continued to live on "the Preston land" after her death, reported that Crook's troops had visited his home and had taken a mare from his stable. Descendants of the Preston family have also preserved the story that enslaved workers at White Thorn helped the family hide its silver and trick Union soldiers into refusing to take a valuable horse. No other account, however, has survived of Union troops visiting any of the Preston plantations in Montgomery County, and no record has survived suggesting that any of the people enslaved on those plantations escaped with Crook. It seems highly unlikely that Union soldiers extracting food and animals from the enemy would have ignored three of the largest plantations along their path through the county. And given the subsequent history of the Prestons and the people they enslaved, it seems equally unlikely that the latter were so loyal to the Prestons that not one of them took the opportunity presented by the Union army to gain his or her freedom. Several clues suggest that the answer to this mystery may be that few of the men enslaved by the Prestons were actually in the county at the time of the invasion.[9]

A postwar deposition by the executor of William Ballard Preston's estate indicated that following Preston's death in 1862, the population of Preston's Henry County plantations included "a large number of women & children who could not be rented out." A similar situation may have existed at Smithfield. Financial records from the estate of William Ballard Preston include a credit for $3,000 dated March 15, 1864, for "hire of negroes at Iron Works," suggesting that some or all of the working-age males at Smithfield may have been hired out that spring. This could also be the reason that billing records of Dr. Henry Ribble, who provided medical services to both Black and White residents of Smithfield from 1862 until 1865, include numerous visits to Black women or children throughout 1864 but none that year to a Black man until August. While inconclusive, the surviving evidence does suggest that perhaps the only Preston workers in the county when Crook arrived were women and children for whom the thought of following the Union column without their husbands and sons may have been too intimidating.[10]

Whatever happened during the spring of 1864, the war clearly did take a number of Black men away from Smithfield and from the families they left behind there. Most of these men had no choice in whether or not to go. Officers in the Confederate army often came from the slave-owning class and were accustomed to enslaved men and women caring for their domestic needs. When these men joined the army, they often took such workers with them to prepare their meals, wash their laundry, clean their quarters, and perform a variety of other chores. James F. Preston had taken Taylor McNorton with him in 1847, when he volunteered to serve in the Mexican War, and did so again in 1861, when he enlisted in the Confederate army and became colonel of the Fourth Virginia Infantry. McNorton was thirty-nine at the time and had family ties to others enslaved on each of the Prestons' Montgomery County plantations. He lived at White Thorn with his brother, Ballard, and his sister, Eliza McNorton Burke. His wife, Syrena, and the couple's three children lived at Solitude as did his sister, Grace, and his brother, Daniel. His parents, William and Catherine, still lived at Smithfield, along with his brothers, Robert and Orville, and his sister, Marsha.[11]

Taylor McNorton may have come back to White Thorn when his owner did late in 1861. Civil War armies were rarely active during the winter, and officers who could often took the opportunity to return home on leave. James F. Preston may have been especially interested in getting away from the army because he had suffered health problems throughout the fall and may have hoped to recover more quickly at home. Instead, his health worsened, and he died in January 1862. Preston's will instructed his widow to free Taylor McNorton or keep him enslaved "as his conduct to me during my continuance in service may deserve." She not only kept him enslaved but kept him in the army as well. In April 1862 Taylor was serving as a cook for Dr. Harvey Black, who had long been a friend of the Prestons and until the war broke out had served as the physician to both White and Black residents of Smithfield, Solitude, and White Thorn. By September, though, McNorton was no longer with Dr. Black, and had probably returned to White Thorn.[12]

Ironically, he arrived just in time to face another chance of being taken into military service. The Confederate army desperately needed laborers, and between October 1862 and March 1863 both the Virginia General Assembly and the Confederate Congress passed legislation authorizing the impressment of slaves to provide them. Under these laws, the governor was authorized to call for slaveholders to provide men between the ages of eighteen and forty-five to work for up to sixty days on fortifications or "other works necessary for the public defense," and the first such call went out that autumn. Montgomery County officials learned in early December 1862 that the county's quota was one hundred men and promptly issued orders to seventy individual slave owners—including the Prestons—to provide from one to eight men each for two months' service building fortifications near Richmond. Five enslaved men were expected to be sent from the estate of William Ballard Preston, one man from James Preston's estate, and three men from Robert Preston's plantation. In all, nine men enslaved by the Prestons were called that month to serve as laborers for the Confederate military, though it is impossible to say how many actually went, who they were, or what they did. Nor is it clear if any were sent in response to four later calls issued from Richmond.[13]

Other enslaved men were leased to Confederate officials. Hiring slaves had been a common and familiar practice in antebellum Virginia, and it continued during the war. During the war, though, it was not just private employers hiring enslaved workers. Government and military officials hired hundreds of men and women to serve as laborers, hostlers, teamsters, industrial workers, hospital workers, and more. William Ballard Preston had leased workers before his death, and his estate did so after he died; at least some of those leased by the estate worked for the Confederate government. Financial records of Preston's estate show a credit of $160 in April 1863 from "Confederate States for hire of Negroes." It is impossible to say, however, who was hired, for how long, or to do what.

The presence of enslaved men working in or for the Confederate military has often led to persistent and inaccurate misconceptions concerning the motives and roles of African Americans and the Confederate war effort. In the late nineteenth and early twentieth centuries, Confederate veterans pointed to these "loyal servants" as evidence that Southern slaves had been devoted to their masters and had willingly supported a way of life destroyed by the Civil War and Reconstruction. More recently, during the late twentieth and early twenty-first centuries, individuals and groups opposed to the Civil Rights movement or resistant to the growing recognition that the Confederate States of America existed to protect slavery and promote White supremacy further distorted the image of enslaved Confederate servants and laborers. Seizing upon the fact that enslaved men living in Confederate camps sometimes wore military clothing and sometimes posed for pictures with the men they served, and that isolated, erroneous reports of armed Black men serving in the Confederate army did sometimes appear during the Civil War, these people and groups distorted history to create a category of "Black Confederates." These are not the "loyal servants" described by Confederate veterans or the African American conscripts forced to dig earthworks for the Confederacy; they are enslaved men who, supposedly, took up arms and actively fought on behalf of the Confederacy.[14]

It is true that during the final weeks of its existence the Confederate government did authorize the recruitment of Black soldiers and may have attracted a handful of recruits.[15] Otherwise, however, "Black Confederates" belong more to the realm of myth than history. Undoubtedly, some African Americans may have willingly supported the Confederacy, and a handful may even have taken up arms in its defense, but to claim that any significant number did so runs counter to nearly all contemporary evidence and modern scholarship. Whether hired, pressed into service, or taken into the army by their masters, few among the thousands of enslaved men and women who worked for the Confederacy did so voluntarily. There is certainly no indication that any of those enslaved by the Prestons ever did. No surviving document or story from either the Preston family or the families of those they held in bondage suggest that anyone enslaved at Smithfield, Solitude, or White Thorn willingly served the Confederacy. A number did, however, serve the Union.

Black men in the Northern states tried to enlist in the Union army as soon as the war broke out but were initially rejected because of their color. Though African Americans had served in previous wars, and continued to serve in the Union navy, the Union army remained all White for the first year of the Civil War. The Lincoln administration worried that states such as Maryland or Kentucky—that permitted slavery but had not seceded—might leave the Union if the federal government seemed to support emancipation or racial equality. As a result, for more than a year after the war began neither free Blacks living in the Northern states nor enslaved Blacks who escaped to Union lines were permitted to enlist in the Union army. Gradually, however, the United States began to challenge slavery more openly. In 1862, Congress abolished slavery in the territories, freed the slaves of men serving the Confederacy and authorized the president to accept Black men to perform "any military or naval service for which they may be found competent." Finally, in January 1863, the Emancipation Proclamation abolished slavery in the rebellious states and announced the government's intention to begin accepting Black men into both the army and navy of the United States. The army was not integrated, though; Black soldiers served in separate units under White officers. Initially, Black soldiers were also paid less than White soldiers and, unlike their White counterparts, were required to pay for their uniforms. Congress ended these financial differences in 1864, but Black soldiers in the Union army continued to face widespread discrimination and skepticism about their fighting ability. In spite of this, thousands of Black men joined the army, and by the war's end they made up approximately 10 percent of the Union army.[16]

At least five men enslaved by the Prestons may have escaped slavery and enlisted in the Union army during the war. Three of the five—Oscar, Thomas, and Othello Fraction—definitely served. Sons of John and Easther Fraction, the three were born at Smithfield between 1834 and 1845. At the death of James Patton Preston, however, they passed to Robert Preston and went to live at Solitude with their parents and several of their siblings. A fourth man, Robert McNorton, claimed to have served with two of the Factions, though no military records have survived to support his claim. McNorton was also born at Smithfield in 1842 and remained there when the estate of James Patton Preston was divided. He undoubtedly knew the Fraction brothers; members of the two families lived together at both Smithfield and Solitude, and Robert's older brother, Orville McNorton, married Easter Jane Fraction, the Fraction brothers' niece. A fifth man, John Anderson, also served in the Union army. Family tradition indicates that he was a slave of Robert T. Preston's and lived at Solitude, though no documentary evidence has yet emerged to show the connection.

Most of the African Americans who served in the Union army were former slaves who joined after escaping to, or with, that army. Almost as soon as the war began, enslaved people in parts of Virginia, Maryland, Kentucky, and Missouri that were occupied by Union troops or near areas that were occupied began escaping to seek protection from those troops. Initially described as "contraband," some were returned to their owners, but many were given sanctuary and employed by the army as laborers and servants. As the war progressed, Union armies invading the Confederacy became magnets attracting thousands of enslaved men and women seeking freedom and protection, and after the Emancipation Proclamation took effect many of the men who arrived this way volunteered to fight for the Union and enlisted in what became the United States Colored Troops (USCT).

Four of the five Smithfield slaves reported to have served in the USCT—Thomas Fraction, Othello Fraction, Robert McNorton, and John Anderson—seem to have escaped slavery when Union troops entered Montgomery County in 1865 and enlisted together in the Fortieth United States Colored Infantry (USCI). In late March 1865, Union cavalry under Major General George Stoneman left Knoxville, Tennessee, on a mission to destroy Confederate equipment, supplies, and infrastructure wherever they found them. After passing through western North Carolina and into southwestern Virginia, the Union column entered Montgomery County from the south and spent several days in Christiansburg, destroying railroad track and bridges east and west of town before moving south again into North Carolina. By the time Stoneman's troops reentered North Carolina, they were accompanied by several hundred former slaves, including a number from Montgomery County. From North Carolina, Stoneman sent many of the formerly enslaved men who had followed him under escort to eastern Tennessee, where they enlisted in the Union army. Among them were four who had been enslaved by Prestons. They arrived in Greenville, Tennessee, and joined the Fortieth USCI in late April 1865.[17]

Oscar Fraction, the older brother of Thomas and Othello, seems to have followed a different path. Medical records of Harvey Black indicate that Oscar was still at Solitude as late as June 1859, when Dr. Black lanced his finger. After that, however, he disappeared from the historical record until September 1864, when he enlisted in the Union army at Circleville, Ohio. It is possible that Oscar made his way to Circleville after escaping Solitude when Union troops invaded Montgomery County in May 1864. Dozens of enslaved men and women followed the Union column as it returned to West Virginia, including a number of men who promptly joined the Union army. When they did so, these men were identified as "volunteers," although they were sometimes recruited by agents dispatched by Northern states and might be credited to the enlistment quotas of those states. Oscar Fraction, however, enlisted as a "substitute volunteer." When the Union began to draft men for military duty in 1863, the Enrollment Act allowed any man drafted to find and hire a substitute to serve in his place. Oscar Fraction was such a substitute. In return for "sufficient consideration paid and delivered" by Thomas D. Cramblit, Fraction agreed to serve one year in Cramblit's place. Cramblit and Fraction must have met to negotiate their agreement before Fraction enlisted, which suggests that Oscar Fraction may have already been living in Ohio when he agreed to serve on behalf of Cramblit. Further evidence of this possibility comes from Fraction's pension application. To support his application, Fraction submitted affidavits from a number of men who knew him and his postwar medical problems. One of these men, William Bowman, described Fraction "at the time he came home from the service." The wording here—"came home"—suggests that Fraction had been living in Ohio before joining the army. Sometime between 1859 and 1864, it seems, Oscar Fraction may have escaped slavery and settled in Ohio, and while living there as a free man he agreed to serve as a substitute for Thomas Cramblit when the latter was drafted.[18]

However they came to be in the army, all of these men spent most of their time serving the Union through garrison duty rather than combat. This was partly because most of them enlisted just as the war was ending. Four of the five joined the Fortieth USCI in April of 1865, the same month that Robert E. Lee and Joseph E. Johnson surrendered the two most important Confederate armies. They and other members of their regiment spent the next year guarding railroad lines and depots in southeastern Tennessee and northeastern Alabama before mustering out in April 1866. The use of Black troops in such support roles was also, however, a result of White Americans' skepticism about how well they would perform in combat. Many Whites doubted that African Americans were brave enough or intelligent enough to serve in combat, so they were often employed away from the front as laborers, teamsters, or guards. Even Oscar Fraction, who enlisted in 1864, spent his time in the Fifteenth USCI, guarding railroad and military installations in and around Nashville, Tennessee. This may not have been glamourous duty, but it was militarily important. And it was dangerous. Disease killed more men than bullets did during the Civil War, and it struck troops everywhere. Oscar Fraction, for example, contracted a severe cough and suffered debilitating respiratory problems for the rest of his life after spending several nights sleeping in rain and snow on a Nashville railroad platform during his time in the army.[19]

Of the five Smithfield men who served in the Union army, only Othello Fraction left a wife behind when he did so. All of the men, however, left family behind, and elsewhere in the Confederacy angry masters sometimes punished the families of enslaved men who joined the Union army by working them harder or feeding them less. Had the war lasted longer, Robert Preston might well have taken such action. Preston was a vindictive man. According to Othello Fraction, one of the men he enslaved, "our master said if any of his 'niggirs' went to the army & came back he would kill them." Such an attitude might well have led Preston to seek revenge on other members of the extended Fraction family if slavery had lasted longer than it did after Thomas and Othello fled.[20]

It did not, though. Less than a month after Thomas and Othello Fraction escaped from Solitude, the Confederacy collapsed and with it, slavery in Montgomery County. No record has come to light describing when or how the momentous word reached Smithfield. It probably came quickly; word of Lee's surrender reached Christiansburg by April 11, two days after it happened, and must have spread rapidly from there. How the word was delivered or received, though, remains unknown. Elizabeth Payne, who lived near Shawsville in eastern Montgomery County, described the end of slavery on her family's plantations in a matter-of-fact way: "The negroes, of course, were freed." Janie Milton, whose great-grandparents were enslaved in the county, recalled an equally mundane announcement; their owner simply announced one day: "'Well you all's set free today." Even William Moon, whose sons were enslaved by the Prestons until 1865, said only "I

was glad at the surrender and glad the colored people got their freedom."
How the news reached those enslaved by the Prestons remains a mystery.[21]

It is hard to imagine, however, that those held in slavery at Smithfield,
Solitude, and White Thorn took the news calmly. It must have brought
a mixture of joy, confusion, and fear. Joy at their liberation from a life in
which every major decision was made for them by their owners, a life in
which families were created and destroyed with no regard for the people
in those families, what they wanted, or how they felt. But liberation also
meant confusion. No one knew exactly what "freedom" meant. Virginia law
had long recognized three classes of people: Whites, who had full legal,
civil, and property rights; slaves, who had none; and free people of color,
who enjoyed few rights and whose privileges had been sharply limited by
the state legislature between 1800 and 1865. The lives and property of free
people of color were protected in antebellum Virginia, but they were also
subject to a variety of restrictions that Whites were not. Although the laws
were often ignored, state law did declare free people of color in Virginia
could only move from one county to another with the consent of public
officials; they were required to register with county officials every three
years and to keep copies of their "free papers" in order to prove their status;
they were barred from preaching, from worshipping without White supervision, from owning firearms without a license, from making or dispensing
medicine, from buying alcohol without the permission of local authorities,
and from selling hard liquor; it was also illegal for anyone to educate them.
Did these same restrictions apply to former slaves freed by the fall of the
Confederacy? If so, would they be enforced more strictly than they had
been against free people of color?

And what of their property and families? Most of the men enslaved by
the Prestons had been farmers all their lives. They certainly had experience
and skill, but they owned none of the material they would need to continue
farming; they had no land, no tools, and no livestock. How would they support their families? Even the houses in which they lived belonged to the
Prestons. Enslaved men had almost certainly built them, and they and their
families had lived in them for years, but they had no legal claim to them.
They may also have made furniture or household goods to use in the quarters and may have been able to buy other goods with money earned selling
vegetables they raised in their gardens, fish or game they caught themselves,
or products they made on their own time. While enslaved, they had enjoyed

no *legal* claim to anything they bought or made for themselves. Now that they were free, did they have any claim to property they had acquired as slaves?

Similarly, enslaved men and women had often been allowed to marry, but their marriages had no legal standing in Virginia. Enslaved couples could be joined or separated as their owners wished; husbands had no authority over their wives' bodies or labor and could protect neither against exploitation by their wives' owners, and parents had no right to protect their children from abuse at the hands of their owners or from being sold to another—more distant—owner. For free people of color, marriage had been a legal limbo. Virginia law established clear procedures for effecting a legal marriage, but they applied only to White marriages. Free people of color had married, and their unions had often been recognized by their White neighbors, but they had no legal standing. What happened, though, when enslaved couples were freed in 1865? Would their marriages be recognized? Would they have any legal standing? Were their children legitimate?

The spring of 1865 brought change to every facet of life for the men and women held in bondage by the Prestons. Slavery was over; what would freedom bring?

5

From Slavery to Freedom

W hen the Confederacy finally collapsed, slave owners in southwest Virginia did little to help those they had enslaved start new lives for themselves. Indeed, as time passed and as Whites in the region came to realize that freedpeople intended to exercise all of the social, economic, and political rights associated with freedom, many Whites took active—sometimes violent—measures to stop them. Nor did state or local governments do much to help African Americans make the transition from slaves to citizens. Most did only what they were required to do and abolished slavery. Even Congress took few meaningful steps to help freedpeople. In March 1865, it acted to provide emergency relief through the Bureau of Refugees, Freedmen, and Abandoned Lands (better known as the Freedmen's Bureau). Though often associated with the promise of "forty acres and a mule," the Freedmen's Bureau rarely provided land, animals, or tools to the freedpeople. Initially, it provided only basic, immediate assistance: "provisions, clothing, and fuel . . . for the immediate and temporary shelter and supply of destitute and suffering refugees and their wives and children." Later legislation did permit the bureau's agents to supervise labor relations between White employers and Black workers and to cooperate with charitable organizations to establish schools for African Americans, but the Freedmen's Bureau was never intended to eliminate the obstacles between former slaves and genuine independence. To a significant degree, freedpeople were on their own.[1]

This was certainly the case in Montgomery County. The Freedmen's Bureau was active there for several years, and a handful of the county's

White residents did take modest steps to help its formerly enslaved residents negotiate the transition to freedom, but freedpeople did most of the work themselves. In the twenty-five years immediately after their emancipation, African Americans in the county worked tirelessly to establish the institutions of a functioning African American community. Chief among these were churches and schools. As described in chapter 3, enslaved workers in Montgomery County had frequently attended and even become members of White-controlled Methodist, Presbyterian, and Baptist congregations. After the Civil War, though, these biracial assemblies quickly divided along racial lines. Black Christians often initiated this separation themselves in order to play a greater role in directing their spiritual lives and shaping the tone of the services they attended. For their part, Whites rarely objected to the departure of Black members from their congregations, for as the local Baptist association declared in 1866: "the Great Author of all created beings has declared that whatever human law may enjoin, or infidel fanaticism may inculcate, the line of demarcation [between the races] is too clearly drawn ever to be obliterated." As a result, between 1867 and 1892 African Americans established at least twenty-two independent congregations in Montgomery County.[2]

Schools were equally important in building a Black community in the county, and many of the Black churches established there after the Civil War also housed schools. Before the war, Virginia law made it a crime to teach any African American—free or enslaved—to read or write. A tiny number of the county's Black residents had learned to read in spite of the law, but the vast majority had not, and when freedom came, they moved quickly to initiate the establishment of schools open to African Americans. Just two months after his arrival, the local agent of the Freedmen's Bureau, Charles Schaeffer, wrote that "the Freed People generally are anxiously waiting for some action to be taken, in regard to the education of their children." And they were not waiting passively. Few of the county's freedpeople were educated enough to serve as teachers themselves, but they could provide school buildings and board for teachers provided by Northern aid societies. "The Freed-people will aid all in their power to support the schools," wrote Schaeffer, "although the great majority of them receive scarcely sufficient wages to supply them with shelter, clothing, and the necessaries of life." With the help of the Freedmen's Bureau and Northern philanthropists, schools for freedpeople began opening in the county early in 1867. By 1870 at least six schools were operating in the county's African American community, and with the state's decision that year to establish public schools for the first time, the number rose steadily over the next two decades. Most of these were one-room primary schools, but by 1885 the school started in Christiansburg in 1867 had developed into the Christiansburg Institute, which offered both primary and secondary education in a range of academic subjects as well as vocational training for both males and females.[3]

Within this emerging African American community, families of the formerly enslaved worked to ensure their own success. This was certainly true of men and women the Prestons had enslaved. Like their peers elsewhere, these freedpeople faced a variety of challenges as they moved to establish new lives. Questions persist about many elements of their transition from slavery to freedom, and parts of their stories may never be known, but enough has survived to offer glimpses of the challenges they faced and of the ways in which they met them. And from these glimpses two facts emerge most clearly. First, no single pattern fits the experience of every individual; people enslaved by the Prestons enjoyed, or endured, a variety of different experiences as they set out to build new lives for themselves as free men and women. Second, however varied those individual experiences were, they often incorporated relationships forged during the years in slavery. As men and women who had been enslaved by the Prestons built new lives for themselves, they often did so with the help of their extended families and the larger community they had formed in the quarters at Smithfield, Solitude, and White Thorn.

Perhaps the clearest example of the wide range of experiences seen among those making the transition from slavery to freedom was that of the Fraction family. Fractions had been enslaved by Prestons since the eighteenth century. John Fraction, patriarch of the family, was in his sixties when slavery ended and was living at Solitude, the plantation of Robert T. Preston. His first wife, Easther, had died a decade earlier, and he had married Fanny Johnson in 1859. By 1865 two of John's younger sons, Wilson and Granville, had died, and at least three others—Oscar, Thomas, and Othello—had escaped slavery and were serving in the Union army. Several other members of the family cannot be located in existing records, but in the spring of 1865 at least nine members of the extended Fraction family were still held in slavery at Smithfield, Solitude, White Thorn, or the Pittsylvania County plantation of George Gilmer. For some of them, the transition to freedom seems to have been smooth and relatively easy. For others, it was more difficult. And for two at least it was a bitter and protracted struggle.[4]

Virginia Fraction's experience was the sort that defenders of slavery sometimes employed to argue that the enslaved had been content with their situation. Virginia was thirty-six years old when she finally gained her freedom. Born at Smithfield, she had been transferred to White Thorn following the death of James Patton Preston and the division of his estate. By then she had already given birth to at least one child, Easter Jane, who was born about 1845. The identity of Easter Jane's father remains a mystery, though, and it is impossible to say whether or not Virginia had been married to him or what happened to him. At White Thorn, she seems to have met and married a man named Dan Caperton, who was probably brought to White Thorn by Sarah Ann Caperton when she married James F. Preston in 1854. He seems to have died by 1865, but he and Virginia had at least four children together, all of whom were living at White Thorn when the Civil War ended. Initially, Virginia retained the name Caperton, but by 1870 she had shortened it to Capers and used that until her death.[5]

While enslaved at White Thorn, Virginia had also developed a close relationship with Sarah Ann Preston, the mistress of White Thorn. Among Preston descendants, Virginia Capers is remembered fondly as "Aunt Ginny"—a trusted family servant. She was probably a house servant or cook during her years in slavery, which would have brought her into frequent contact with Sarah Ann. The two women were nearly the same age; both were widowed at about the same time and left to raise young children on their own; and in 1865 both had to deal with the sudden transformation of the only world they had known for much of their adult lives. Despite the obvious differences between them in class, race, and situation, the women had much in common, and they seem to have forged a relationship that lasted almost thirty years and ended only when Virginia Capers died in 1891. After gaining her freedom, Virginia seems never to have left White Thorn. She appears on an 1867 census of freedpeople in the county as a servant working for Sarah Ann Preston and on the 1870 and 1880 federal censuses as a cook or servant in Preston's household. When she died, the first provision in her will declared: "I wish my two granddaughters Madeline and Rachel to be bound to Mrs. Sarah Preston untill they are twenty one years of age, and specially recommend them to her care." According to family tradition, she was then buried in the Preston family cemetery at Smithfield.[6]

The experience of Virginia Capers's brothers, Thomas and Othello Fraction, could not have been more different. Like Virginia, Thomas and Othello were born at Smithfield, but they were later moved following the death of James Patton Preston. The brothers, both children when Preston's estate was divided, went to Robert Preston's Solitude with their parents, their brothers Oscar and Wilson, and their sister Chloe. Solitude remained the brothers' home for the next twenty years, though they may have been hired out or pressed into government service during that time. They may also have spent time on one of William Ballard Preston's Henry County plantations given that in the spring of 1864 Othello Fraction married Mary Carr, who was born in Henry County and belonged to the estate of William Ballard Preston. Solitude was the brothers' home, though, and it was from Solitude that they escaped slavery in April 1865.[7]

As described in chapter 4, Thomas and Othello Fraction were probably among those formerly enslaved men and women who followed General George Stoneman's cavalry out of Montgomery County in April 1865. Within two weeks, a number of these men, including the Fraction brothers had reached Greenville, Tennessee, where they enlisted in the Union army for three years' service. Thomas and Othello do not seem to have gone through any basic training facility before being assigned to the Fortieth United States Colored Infantry, and by the end of June they were on active duty with the regiment. Othello, the younger of the two, remained a private, but Thomas was promoted to sergeant in July and held that rank until January 1, 1866. He was then reduced in rank to private, but neither his service record nor his pension record explains why. His service record says only that it was a result of Special Order No. 1 from regimental headquarters, which suggests that the change may have been a result of adjustments made as troops were mustered out and units consolidated following the end of hostilities rather than any improper behavior on Thomas's part, but that cannot be confirmed.[8]

In February 1866, Thomas and Othello Fraction were granted thirty-day furloughs and set off to visit family in Montgomery County. In the months since their escape from Solitude, the brothers had learned that Robert Preston had threatened to kill any of his former slaves who joined the army and then returned to the plantation. Officials of the Freedmen's Bureau later wrote that the Fractions "did not suppose he [Preston] would carry out the threat," but Bureau officials reported that Thomas had written to Preston that "in case of their return, they would not quietly submit to be fired upon, but would be prepared to defend themselves." Whether they believed Preston or not, the Fraction brothers were determined to go back to Solitude in order to help their father. John Fraction had remained at Solitude after gaining his freedom. He was then in his mid-sixties and had lived his entire life on the Prestons' land. His wife, Fanny, was also in her sixties and like John, had spent her life in slavery. The couple had few viable alternatives when freedom came, so they remained at Solitude, where John worked for Robert Preston in exchange for "board & clothes." Now, according to another Montgomery County planter, the Fraction brothers had learned that Preston had ordered their father out of the house that he and Fanny occupied at Solitude, and the brothers were determined to help their parents if they could.[9]

On February 27, 1866, shortly after Thomas and Othello arrived at their father's cabin, another freedman warned the brothers that Preston "had armed himself to do them bodily harm." Preston had also enlisted his son-in-law, Robert Stark Means, in the effort, and the two men—both Confederate veterans—had armed themselves with pistols before going in search of the Fractions. Rather than risk a confrontation in which their father and stepmother might also be at risk, the brothers "strapped on their knapsacks" and started to leave. They had not gotten far, however, before Preston and Means caught up with them. In the legal proceedings that followed, each side blamed the other for firing first. The Fractions testified that Preston began the fray by raising his pistol and "taking deliberate aim" at them but that his pistol misfired. Preston, on the other hand, admitted that he had raised his pistol because "he fully believed the boys had malicious intentions against him" but denied pulling the trigger until fired upon. However it began, the confrontation rapidly escalated into a skirmish in which both sides discharged their weapons repeatedly, and nearly a dozen shots were fired. In the exchange of gunfire Thomas Fraction was wounded in the right leg, and with Thomas disabled, both he and Othello were "secured." They were then taken to Salem and held in the jail there for three months while the army investigated. Ultimately, the investigating officer reported that the brothers had acted in self-defense, and Brigadier General Alfred H. Terry, commanding the Department of Virginia, ordered their release in June 1866.[10]

Meanwhile, the Fortieth USCI had been mustered out that April, so Thomas and Othello Fraction returned briefly to Tennessee, where they were honorably discharged from the army, and immediately returned to

Montgomery County to begin their lives as civilians. They settled near Blacksburg but did not return to Solitude. Robert Preston had barred them from "trespassing on his premises," and the brothers respected that order. They could not, however, avoid Preston entirely. John and Fanny Fraction were both members of the Methodist Church in Blacksburg, and while neither Thomas nor Othello were members, they did sometimes attend services there. On one occasion when they did so, Preston met them at the door of the church with a gun and "ordered them immediately to leave." According to reports filed by the Freedmen's Bureau, Preston announced "that he was the proprietor there, and that they and him could not worship in the same church, nor live in the same town together—and threatened to shoot them if they did obey his order." The brothers left and, according to the Freedmen's Bureau, "have not been at the church since."[11]

Preston was not done, though. In September 1866, a grand jury in Christiansburg, acting "at the insistence of Mr. Preston," offered presentments against Thomas and Othello Fraction for the attempted murder of Robert Preston in connection with the February shoot-out. The circuit court, however, seems to have issued no warrants for their arrest, and no action was taken on the matter until February 1867. Finally, a single judge issued a bench warrant for the Fractions' arrest. On February 6, the brothers were both working, "one building a log house for his family—the other in the field," when they were arrested by the sheriff and taken to Christiansburg for examination. Their examination was postponed several times, however, leaving the men in jail for more than a week. Then the examining magistrate refused to grant them bail, reportedly because he was "affraid to take action in the case, lest he might offend 'Col.' Preston." Federal officials were angered by the arrest and concerned about the Fractions' fate. J. H. Remington, the Freedmen's Bureau superintendent for southwest Virginia, called it "a vengeful and malicious prosecution" and concluded that "the chances of justice at the hands of civil authorities appear to be very slight." [12]

After ten days in jail, the brothers were finally granted a hearing and an opportunity to tell their side of the story. The presiding magistrate listened to their testimony but still ordered them to stand trial. He did, however, allow their release on bail, and a White neighbor provided security on their bonds to appear.[13] Legal proceedings then dragged on for another three months. Preston was said to be "very anxious to have the boys convicted and sent to the penitentiary," but their trial was postponed repeatedly. Finally, the court heard their case on May 6, 1867, and dismissed it almost immediately. The judge declared that the Fractions had already been acquitted by the military and could not be tried again on the same charge. Therefore, the warrant against them was quashed, and the brothers were discharged.[14]

Dismissal of the murder charges against Thomas and Othello Fraction finally brought an end to their ordeal at the hands of Robert Preston. By the summer of 1867, if not before, the entire family had left Solitude. Thomas, his parents, and his sister Chloe settled on the farm of Michael Kipps, who lived several miles west of Blacksburg. John and Thomas worked there as farmers for wages, while Chloe worked as a washerwoman. Fanny Fraction was also with the family but was not working and appears as "crippled" on the census of freedpeople taken that year. Othello Fraction moved even farther out of Robert Preston's orbit. He and his wife, Mary, moved to Christiansburg. They appear on the 1867 census as servants working for Thomas Wilson, a Christiansburg hotel owner, and in October of that year Othello voted in the Christiansburg precinct. Listed with Othello and Mary on the 1867 census is a fourteen-year-old boy named Willis Fraction, whose identity remains a mystery.[15]

Nor were the Fractions likely to encounter Robert Preston at church again. Dozens of African Americans, most of them enslaved, had been members of the Methodist church in Blacksburg during the antebellum era. The practice of Blacks and Whites worshipping at the same time, however, masked an underlying current of racial tension that was common among churches in American South. As Robert Preston so clearly demonstrated, White members often saw their Black "brothers" and "sisters" as subordinates and made it clear that they needed to remember their place. Black members, for their part, must have known how Whites felt about them. They were frequently seated in separate—more remote—sections of the church, were never offered positions of authority in their congregations, and repeatedly heard sermons that were more about obedience than love. It is hardly surprising then that Southern churches rapidly split along racial lines following the abolition of slavery. Black Christians preferred churches in which they were truly welcome, and White members were happy to see them go. In the case of Blacksburg's Methodist congregation, the separation came during the summer of 1867. John Wesley Diggs, a minister of the African Methodist Episcopal (AME) Church, visited Blacksburg for the first time in May and June. He preached, performed at least one marriage, and "gathered forty" during his time in town. Two months later, when Blacksburg Methodists held their quarterly meeting, the minutes reported: "Since the last quarter 4 have been received by certificates. Coloured members withdrawn." No early membership lists from the Blacksburg AME Church have survived, so it is impossible to say if the Fractions worshipped there. They certainly do not appear, however, in any records of the Blacksburg Methodist Church after 1866.[16]

In the years that followed, the Fractions continued the process of making their freedom real. They were already working and earning their livelihoods as free men, and in October 1867 John and Othello Fraction had voted in the election of delegates to the state constitutional convention—the first time Black men had ever been allowed to vote in Virginia. By then Othello and Thomas also had the wherewithal to gain the ultimate mark of freedom— land of their own. While awaiting dismissal of the murder charges against them in 1867, the brothers had received final settlements from the army for back pay and enlistment bonuses due to them for their service: $158.34 for Othello and $137.67 for Thomas. Whites in Montgomery County were often willing to sell land to freedpeople, and by the late 1860s several formerly enslaved individuals had already purchased land there. The Fraction brothers, however, had apparently had enough of Montgomery County and decided to make a fresh start for themselves in Roanoke County.[17]

The Fraction family had no obvious connection to Roanoke County before moving there. Thomas and Othello, of course, had been jailed there for several months in 1866, but that hardly seems a likely recommendation. Nevertheless, Salem, the county seat, did have a number of attractions. It was just twenty-five miles from Christiansburg and connected by both road and rail, making it possible to keep in touch with friends and family in Montgomery County. And as the county seat and a railroad town, Salem offered a wider range of employment opportunities for both men and women than were available in more rural communities. Whatever the appeal, between 1868 and 1870 at least five members of the Fraction family relocated to Salem. Thomas did so in November 1868; Othello by 1869; and John, Ellen, and Chloe by 1870. They and their families all settled within two blocks of one another in a new African American community that emerged in Salem after the Civil War. The land on which this community arose had been part of Dropmore, the plantation of Nicholas Burwell, until Burwell died in 1866. His executor then divided much of the land into small tracts and sold it

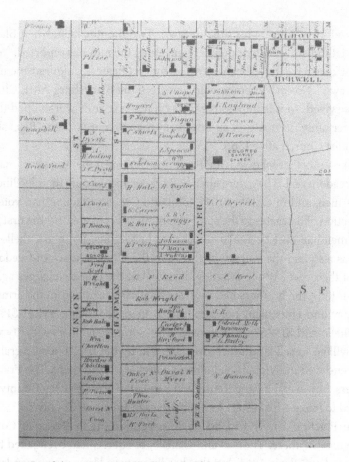

Map of the Water Street community in Salem about 1880 showing lots occupied by Thomas Fraction, Chloe Fraction Shorts, and
Ellen Fraction Ragland. (Salem Museum)

through two public auctions in June 1868 and May 1869. A number of the
lots in what was initially called Dropmore Estate were sold to freedpeople
and formed the core of a neighborhood extending several blocks south of
Main Street along Union, Chapman, and Water Streets and the cross streets
between them. This eventually became known as the Water Street community and grew to include dozens of Black homes as well as churches, schools,
and businesses serving and owned by Salem's African American residents.
Water Street was soon the center of Black life in Salem and remained a distinct community until it gradually evolved into a less racially distinctive
neighborhood once legal segregation ended in the 1960s.[18]

Thomas Fraction was the first of his family known to have moved to Roanoke County. He moved to Salem in November 1868. Two years later, in July 1870, he married Isabella Calloway (née Tate). Isabella was born in Franklin County, Virginia, in 1844 and married a man named Lewis Calloway in 1866. That marriage fell apart almost immediately, though witnesses disagreed as to why. Either abandoned or absconding, Isabella had then moved to Salem and gone to work as a chambermaid in a local hotel. She reportedly had a child by Lewis Calloway, a daughter called Jennie, and later census records for Isabella and Thomas Fraction do include a daughter, Virginia, born three or four years before Isabella's marriage to Thomas. Isabella later claimed that by the time she met Thomas she had heard that Lewis Calloway had been killed in an industrial accident, and when she married Fraction the license identified her as a widow. Calloway later turned up alive, though, and the federal government ultimately concluded that Isabella had no legal right to Thomas's army pension after he died because she had still been legally married to Lewis Calloway when she married Fraction.[19]

None of this, however, seems to have surfaced while Thomas was alive; he and Isabella lived quietly in Salem for almost twenty-five years until his death in 1892. No record has yet surfaced to show that Thomas ever bought property in Salem, but a map of Salem produced about 1880 identifies a lot on Chapman Street as the home of "T. Fraction." Thomas and Isabella may have rented a house and lot there or may have been buying them over time and did not receive a deed until the sale was complete. County records do indicate that in 1891, shortly before Thomas's death, Isabella purchased a lot on Chapman Street, and her application to continue receiving Thomas's pension after he died reported that she owned "a small house and lot here in Salem Va. worth about $150.00." Thomas seems to have accepted Isabella's daughter as his own, and the couple had at least four children together between 1871 and 1883. Thomas worked a variety of jobs during his years in Salem. According to the federal census, he was working as a farmhand in 1870, while county birth records identify him as a laborer throughout the 1870s. The 1880 census called him a "hotel hand," and his application for an army pension, filed in 1884, describes a shoulder injury he sustained "coupling a car" while employed by the Norfolk & Western Railroad. Thomas Fraction died on December 13, 1892. A brief announcement in the *Roanoke Times* declared that he had died "after a long illness" but offered no further details. He left Isabella a widow with a young son, Frank (age nine). She and

Frank then moved to Baltimore to live with Thomas and Isabella's daughter, Mary Ellen, and her husband, Thomas Diggs. Isabella died there in 1918.[20]

Othello Fraction remained in Montgomery County for a year after his brother moved to Salem. He worked at the Yellow Sulphur Springs Resort in 1868 and 1869 and moved to Salem late in 1869. There he and his wife, Mary, purchased a lot in the Water Street community about a block from the one on which Thomas and Isabella lived. They immediately sold part of their land to trustees of the Bethel AME Church and another part to a man named Moses Johnson. On the remaining portion, they hired Robert and Walter McNorton to build a house for them. Othello knew both of the McNortons quite well; they had also been enslaved at Smithfield, and Walter had recently worked with Othello at Yellow Sulphur Springs. Tax records suggest that Othello and Mary Fraction remained in Salem only until 1871, and it seems they may have lost both their house and land when they were unable to cover their debt to the McNortons. It is impossible to say exactly when the couple left Salem or where they went immediately. By 1878, however, they were living in Baltimore, and in 1883 they purchased a house and lot in Cross Keys, one of the city's oldest African American neighborhoods. They spent the rest of their lives in Baltimore, where Othello worked as a waiter or manual laborer and was active in Baltimore County's Republican party. The couple had at least one child together, a daughter named Eva, who was born in 1886 and lived into the early twentieth century. Mary Fraction died in February 1891, and Othello remarried in 1901. His second wife, Savilla Scott Smith, was the granddaughter of Aquila Scott, an early settler of Cross Keys and the founder of St. John's Church, one of Baltimore's first Black churches. It was also a second marriage for Savilla, though in later years it came out that she had never actually divorced her first husband, who was still alive when she married Othello Fraction. Savilla and Othello had a son, Othello Roosevelt Fraction, who was born in January 1902, but he died in 1909 after a cut on his heel became infected. By then, Othello was also dead, stricken by "apoplexy" in January 1904. Savilla lived on until 1919, when she too died of apoplexy.[21]

John Fraction may have moved to Salem with Othello in 1869. He does not appear on the 1868 or 1869 tax rolls in either Montgomery or Roanoke Counties but is on the 1870 tax roll in Salem. He did not remain in Salem for long, though. He left in 1871 or 1872, perhaps at the same time Othello left, and was back in Blacksburg by March 1872. He was still in Montgomery

County in 1874, but the tax roll for that year is the last record yet found of John Fraction, suggesting that he died late in 1874 or early in 1875.[22]

Ellen Fraction also settled in the Water Street community about the time her brothers did. Following the death of James Patton Preston in 1843, Ellen had passed to Preston's daughter, Catharine, and was taken to Pittsylvania County when Catharine married George H. Gilmer. There Ellen married Armistead Ragland, also enslaved by the Gilmers, in December 1856. After gaining their freedom, the couple moved to Montgomery County long enough to register their marriage on the cohabitation register in 1866, but by 1870 had settled in Roanoke County. On the federal census that year, which was taken in September, the Raglands were living in Salem Township, where Armistead worked as a farm laborer. Two months later, though, Ellen and Armistead Ragland purchased lot number two in the Dropmore Estate—just a block from Ellen's brothers, Thomas and Othello. The Raglands would remain in the Water Street community for more than 30 years. Indeed, they seem to have been rather prominent members of the community. Armistead operated a grocery for at least some of the time they lived on Water Street and served as a trustee of Bethel AME Church—the same congregation to which Othello Fraction had sold part of his lot in 1869. The couple had no children of their own but Virginia Fraction Capers's granddaughters, Rachel and Madeline, were living with them in 1900. Ellen died in 1902 and Armistead in 1907.[23]

Chloe Fraction also seems to have relocated to Salem in 1870.[24] Chloe was the daughter of John and Easther Fraction and, like her parents and several of her siblings, seems to have passed to Robert T. Preston when the estate of James Patton Preston was distributed. Chloe seems to have married a man named Samuel Shorts about 1850 and had at least four children with him between 1851 and 1863. Neither Samuel nor any of the children appear, however, on the 1867 census of freedpeople in Montgomery County, which shows Chloe living with her parents and her brother Thomas. Three years later, though, the federal census shows Chloe Shorts living with three children in Salem, and by 1873 she had begun to purchase lot number ninety-two in the Dropmore Estate, just one lot away from Thomas and Isabella Fraction's lot number ninety-four. There she remained for some twenty years, working as a servant and raising her children: Samuel Jr., Rebecca, Adelia, and Flora. Early in the twentieth century she moved a few blocks west to live with Adelia and her husband, John

Patterson, and their family. Chloe Fraction Shorts died in 1912 and was buried in Salem's "African Cemetery."[25]

Even Oscar Fraction, the third of John and Easther's surviving sons, may have considered settling in Salem in the early 1870s. Oscar had escaped to Ohio before or during the Civil War and enlisted there as a substitute in the Union army. After the war, he returned to Ohio and settled near Albany, in Athens County, where he worked as a farm laborer and reportedly lived with a Black woman "as man and wife." At some point in the early 1870s, Oscar travelled to Salem. He may have gone just to visit his father and siblings or may have been investigating the possibility of moving back to Virginia and settling near family in the Water Street community. While in Salem, he met a woman named Fanny Lovely. Fanny was married to Elijah Lovely and seems to have been living just a few doors from Chloe Fraction Shorts, which may be how Oscar met her. One surviving account claims that Oscar did not know Fanny was married, and a letter that Oscar wrote to her was addressed to "Miss Fanny Lovely." The text of that letter, however, expressed concern about "trouble hereafter"—suggesting that he did know her marital status. All that is certain, though, is that Oscar Fraction and Fanny Lovely became attracted to one another. After returning to Ohio early in 1873, Oscar wrote Fanny, "if you still remain in mind as you was when I saw you last you may come as soon as you can make it convenient you must leave every thing satisfactory so that they wont be know hereafter so that they will be know trouble hereafter." Fanny's reply has been lost, but it must have been positive because shortly afterwards Oscar sent her a postal money order for $25. The next day Fanny left Salem for Ohio, and three days later, on March 11, 1873, she married Oscar Fraction in Athens County, Ohio.[26]

After Fanny left Salem, Elijah Lovely found under their mattress the letters Oscar had sent her. He then contacted Augustus Palmer, the postmaster in Albany, to ask what he knew of the situation. It was Palmer who reported that Fraction had claimed not to know Fanny Lovely was married. He also reported that Fraction was now "very much alarmed for fear he would be prosecuted," which probably explains why the newlyweds left Athens County soon after they were married. According to Palmer, they had reportedly gone to the farm of Samuel Barnes, a Black man living in Kanawha County, West Virginia, and they seem never to have returned to Athens County. They did return to Ohio in 1874, but they settled in Kenton, more than one hundred miles from Athens County. There Oscar worked as a farmhand and did odd jobs for people in town, though asthma and respiratory problems related to his military service sometimes made it difficult for him to work. Still, he earned enough to purchase several lots in Kenton, was active in the local AME church, and gained a reputation as a good worker and a worthy man. In later years, this helped him regain his military pension. The Bureau of Pensions ruled in 1893 that Oscar's disability had "ceased to exist in a pensionable degree" and stopped the $6 per month he had been receiving since 1890. In seeking its restoration, Oscar submitted a letter of support from Congressman Luther M. Strong. As a lawyer living in Kenton, Strong had frequently hired Oscar to do odd jobs for him; now, as a member of Congress, he wrote the pension bureau that Oscar Fraction was "one of the best and most reliable colored men I ever knew." With Strong's support, Oscar regained his pension in 1894 and continued receiving it until his death in January 1897. Fanny remarried within a few months and lived into the second decade of the twentieth century.[27]

For the Moon family, the transition to freedom was much smoother than it was for the Fractions. The family patriarch, William Moon, had been a free man of color for almost thirty years before his sons were freed. He had never acquired land of his own, but "farming on the Preston farm" he had earned enough by 1863 for him to have his own livestock and household furniture, which placed him among the wealthier free people of color in Montgomery County that year. William Moon did not specify on which Preston farm he was living before the Civil War, but it was probably Solitude. Tax records from the late 1860s show that he was living then at Robert T. Preston's, and it seems likely that he had been before the war as well. His sons had all been enslaved at Smithfield until the death of James Patton Preston in 1843, but at the division of Preston's estate, at least three—Preston, Saunders, and Frank—had gone to Pittsylvania County, with Preston's daughter, Catharine Jane Preston Gilmer. In 1865, the oldest of Moon's sons, Hiram, was in his early forties, while the youngest, Frank, was in his mid-twenties. Frank was certainly married by then and was the father of at least one child. Hiram and Saunders may also have been married at the time of their emancipation, though it is impossible to be certain from the existing records. Like most freedpeople, the Moon brothers began their new lives with few resources, but the property and experience of their father may have provided a foundation on which his sons could begin to build new lives following their emancipation.[28]

Shortly after gaining his freedom, Frank Moon brought his family to Montgomery County to live with his father. It is impossible to be certain just when the family moved, but they had certainly done so by the summer of 1866, when Frank and his wife Lucy registered their marriage with Freedmen's Bureau officials in Montgomery County. They also registered their son Daniel, who was then three years old, and their newborn son, William, named after his grandfather. The family probably began living with William Sr. immediately upon moving to Montgomery County, as this would have provided them with housing while offering assistance to William, who was then more than eighty years old. Frank and his family were certainly living with William by the summer of 1867, when a census of the county's freedpeople found them living together and all working for Robert T. Preston. Frank was identified as a farmer with a lease from Preston, while Lucy was doing laundry for wages, and William Sr. worked as a farmhand for wages.[29]

This multigenerational household remained together for more than a decade, though its composition changed over time. According to the 1870 census, William Sr. was still living with Frank, Lucy, and their children, who now included a daughter, Louise, born in 1868. Both Frank and William were still identified as farmworkers, and it seems the family was still living on land that belonged to Robert T. Preston. The census does not show this conclusively, but the Moons were listed just two households after Preston on the census, suggesting proximity, and William told the Southern Claims Commission in 1877: "I live on Preston land." Living with the Moons in 1870 was Cynthia Franklin, a widow with two daughters of her own. Like the Moon brothers, Cynthia had been enslaved at Smithfield. She appears on the estate inventory of James Patton Preston as a twelve-year-old and, as a child, had no doubt played with the younger Moons, including Frank. In the subsequent division of Preston's estate, Cynthia had gone to White Thorn with James F. Preston. She and her daughters, Hellis and Henrietta, were still living at White Thorn when Preston died in 1862, though nothing is known of Cynthia's husband, if she had one. Following their emancipation, Cynthia and her daughters remained in Montgomery County, and by 1867 Cynthia was working alongside Lucy Moon as a laundress for Robert T. Preston. The Franklins may also have been living with the Moons by then; it is impossible to say for sure, but they certainly were in 1870. Nor is it possible to say how long the Franklins remained with the Moons. Hellis and Henrietta Franklin both married by 1874 and probably went to live with their husbands, and by 1880 Cynthia Franklin was living with Henrietta and Henrietta's husband, David Hickman.[30]

Frank and Lucy Moon had at least two more daughters together—Eliza, born in 1873, and Lucy, born in 1876. Lucy's birth, however, may have killed her mother because Frank Moon, identified as a widower, married Virginia Tatem, a widow, in December 1876. The 1880 census shows their blended family. Frank and Jane Moon were living with four of Frank's children and Jane's son, Jonathan. The census also suggests that Frank's father, William Moon, had died by 1880. He was still alive in early 1878, when he applied for compensation from the Southern Claims Commission for a horse seized by Union troops in 1864. After that, however, no record of William Moon has yet been found. Frank's health was failing too. The 1880 census reported that he had scrofula—enlarged lymph nodes—and was blind. A year later, in fact, the county Board of Supervisors voted to provide him modest financial support because he was "entirely blind and has a considerable family to support." The last known reference to Frank Moon is a list of Montgomery County voters compiled in 1883. It indicates that Frank lived in the Prices Fork precinct, suggesting that the family may finally have moved off Preston land after William died. Frank probably died sometime during the 1880s.[31]

Hiram Moon, Frank's eldest brother, also lived in Montgomery County after gaining his freedom. It is unclear whether Hiram had gone to Pittsylvania County when the estate of James Patton Preston was divided or had remained in Montgomery County on one of the Preston plantations, but he was certainly in Montgomery County by March of 1867. He signed a contract that month to work for Floyd Wall, whose farm was just a few miles west of the Preston land on which Frank and William Moon were living. As a result, Hiram could also offer and receive family support as he began life as a freedman. Later that year, he was included on a census of freedpeople in the county and shown with a wife, Jane, though it is unclear when or where the couple married. Nor is it clear where the couple's daughter, Judy Pate, was living as she appears on neither the county's 1867 census of freedpeople nor the 1870 federal census. When she married Edward (Ned) Vandross in 1872, the marriage license reported that she was born in Montgomery County and identified Hiram Moon as her father, but her surname suggests that he may have been her stepfather. Hiram died sometime during the 1870s, and Jane (called Ginny) went to live with Judy and Ned until her death early in the twentieth century.[32]

Saunders and Preston Moon chose to remain in or near Pittsylvania County after gaining their freedom. They may have visited Montgomery County, but there is no evidence that either lived there after the Civil War. Saunders married Ellen Johnson probably about the same time he gained his freedom, and the couple's first child, Mary, was born in 1866. Saunders and Ellen Moon went on to have at least three more children before Ellen's death in 1885. Saunders farmed ten acres he owned in Callands, a rural community in Pittsylvania County, and also owned property in Chatham, the county seat, where he died sometime between 1900 and 1910. Preston Moon spent his post-emancipation years farming and doing odd jobs in Bedford and Campbell Counties, adjacent to Pittsylvania, and died in Campbell County sometime between 1920 and 1930. His only documented marriage was to Lucy Lee in 1876, but census data indicates that he had at least two children born before 1876, so Lucy may have been his second wife. The couple had another three children, at least, between 1876 and 1882, and remained together until Preston's death, sometime between 1920 and 1930. Lucy died in 1930.[33]

Less is known about the Saunders family after emancipation. What is known suggests that family members remained close to one another in Montgomery County for as long as they can be traced. Margaret (Peggy) Dandridge Saunders had probably been born at Smithfield about 1801 and was taken to White Thorn when the estate of James Patton Preston was divided. She was still living there with two adult daughters—Amanda and Edmonia—when freedom came in 1865. She was then joined by her husband Richard, whose last owner had lived in Botetourt County, and Richard was working for Sarah Preston in 1867. He also voted that year, along with at least a dozen men formerly enslaved by the Prestons. Neither Richard nor Peggy appears in any known record after 1867, though, which suggests that both may have died soon after that date. Of the couple's eleven children named on the 1843 inventory of James Patton Preston's estate, just three can be found after 1865. Robert, a widower, was at Smithfield when slavery ended and two years later was working for shares on the farm of Byrd Linkous, several miles west of Smithfield. With him in 1867 was his son Wesley, though whether or not Wesley had also been enslaved at Smithfield cannot be determined. Robert married Dolly Ellis in January 1870 and later that year the family was farming near Christiansburg. The 1880 census shows Robert and Dolly were farming west of Blacksburg, though Wesley does not appear, and none of the family can be located after that. Amanda Saunders, like her mother, initially stayed at White Thorn after gaining her freedom, working there as a servant for Sarah Preston. By 1870, she was living with Virginia Fraction Capers and was still working as a "house servant"—probably for Sarah Preston. After that, Amanda Saunders vanished from the historical record. Edmonia Saunders was living with her brother Robert in 1867 and in 1870 was working as a cook for Lucinda Preston at Smithfield. In 1880, Edmonia was a "House Keeper" in the home of Henry Johnson, a Black farmworker living west of Blacksburg with his wife and children. After that, she too vanished from any known record.[34]

Like the Fractions, the Moons, and the Saunders, members of the McNorton family often worked together in making the transition from slavery to freedom, and the McNortons may have been the most successful of all the Smithfield families at making this transition. William and Catherine McNorton had been enslaved at Smithfield since the early nineteenth century, and by the late antebellum era theirs was the largest family among those enslaved by the Prestons. When the estate of James Patton Preston was inventoried in 1843, sixteen of the ninety-one enslaved individuals identified were members of the McNorton family. The family continued to grow between 1843 and 1865, though during those years it was divided among the three Preston plantations in Montgomery County and the Gilmer plantation in Pittsylvania County. Neither William nor Catherine McNorton lived to see freedom themselves, and a number of their children had died or been sold by 1865, but at least twenty-nine of the couple's children or grandchildren were set free when slavery was finally abolished in Virginia.[35] Following their emancipation, Frank McNorton remained in Pittsylvania County, and Grace McNorton left Montgomery County for West Virginia, but five McNorton siblings settled in Montgomery County and remained there for most of their lives. They bought land near one another and wove a network of family connections through which to support one another.

Taylor, the eldest of the surviving McNorton siblings, was living at White Thorn when slavery ended. By then, he had been married to Syrena Montague for fifteen years, and the couple had at least five children. It is unclear, though, where Syrena and the children were living in 1865. Medical records suggest they lived at Solitude, but on the cohabitation register Syrena identified her last owner as Sarah Preston, who owned White Thorn. Wherever they ended their lives in slavery, they began their new lives as freedpeople at White Thorn. A census taken during the spring of 1867 shows Taylor working as farmer, with a lease from Sarah Preston, and living with him were Syrena and five children between the ages of three and twelve.[36]

The family seems to have left White Thorn by 1870, and may have done so to escape harassment by Sarah Preston's nephew and neighbor, Waller R. Preston. The eldest son of William Ballard Preston, Waller lived at Smithfield, just east of White Thorn. He had spent most of the war years serving in the Confederate army and during the early years of Reconstruction was a thoroughly unreconstructed rebel who clashed frequently with local officials of the Freedmen's Bureau. One of the most common sources of conflict was the way in which Preston treated Black men who joined the Union League, a national organization that encouraged freedmen to support the Republican party. When the league opened a branch in Montgomery County in 1867, Taylor McNorton joined, and shortly afterwards Preston caught two of Taylor's sons on his property and whipped them for "trespassing." The boys—most likely Taylor's two eldest sons, Edward Patton and Hugh Fleming—were probably just crossing Preston's land on their way somewhere else, but Preston used them as a vehicle to punish their father for his political activity. He also made clear that he would do it again if they—or any other freedpeople—crossed his land. Charles Schaeffer, who oversaw the Freedmen's Bureau in Montgomery County, reported to his superiors: "Mr. Preston states publicly that he will not allow one of *them* to come on his place."[37]

Waller Preston's behavior notwithstanding, Taylor and Syrena maintained good relations with Sarah Preston and her children, but by 1870 they had moved their family slightly farther from Smithfield and by 1876 had moved to Cambria, a community just outside of Christiansburg that had grown up around the railroad station and was home to a number of African American families. Syrena bought a parcel of land near the depot in 1876, though the deed was actually delivered to Taylor, and the couple seems to have lived there until their deaths (Syrena sometime before 1900 and Taylor by 1910). Initially, Taylor continued to work in farming, but as he grew older he took up barbering. He also applied for a pension on the basis of his service during the Mexican War. Congress authorized the payment of pensions to veterans of the Mexican War in 1887, and Taylor applied almost immediately on the basis of his service as a cook in Captain James F. Preston's Company of the First Virginia Volunteers. When the War Department reported that it could not find his name on any regimental rolls, he submitted a second affidavit with a letter of support from Hugh Preston, the son of James and Sarah Preston. Preston testified that he had known Taylor McNorton and of his service in his father's company "ever since I can remember" and described McNorton as "a most worthy man, who should be supported by the government." It was not enough, though. Taylor McNorton had gone to Mexico as a servant of James Preston, and the Bureau of Pensions determined that he had never been "enlisted in the military or naval service of the United States." His claim, therefore, was rejected on the grounds that he had not been "*duly* enlisted."[38]

Taylor and Syrena McNorton also remained active in the Methodist church after gaining their freedom. Both had been members of the church since 1862, at least. They had originally belonged to the congregation in Christiansburg but by 1863 had "removed to Blacksburg," where their sons Edward Patton and Hugh Fleming were baptized on September 6. They do not appear in any record of the Blacksburg congregation after that, however, and may have joined the AME congregation that emerged in Blacksburg during the summer of 1867. By the time Taylor and Syrena moved to Cambria in the mid-1870s, the Christiansburg congregation in which they had previously worshipped had also divided along racial lines and a new "Colored Methodist Church" had taken shape. Unfortunately, no membership records of that new church have survived. The Colored Methodist Church then seems to have reorganized during the 1880s as a result of financial difficulties, and by 1891 Taylor McNorton was a trustee of the new congregation—known then as the "Methodist Episcopal Church (Colored)."[39]

Taylor's brother, Walter McNorton, settled close to Taylor and Syrena, about two miles north of Cambria. As an adolescent, Walter had been taken to Pittsylvania County following the death of James Patton Preston and Catharine Preston's marriage to George H. Gilmer. There he trained as a carpenter and married Eliza Perry, also enslaved by the Gilmers. Almost immediately after gaining his freedom, Walter McNorton brought his family and his carpentry skills to Montgomery County to live. He and Eliza registered their marriage there in 1866 and the following year appeared on a census of freedpeople in the county. At that time they were living four miles north of Christiansburg, and both Walter, a carpenter, and Eliza, a seamstress, were working for Rice D. Montague, a prominent local businessman. By 1869, though, Walter seems to have gone into business for himself; that summer Othello Fraction hired him to build a house in Salem. Walter

McNorton continued working as a carpenter for at least thirty years and was quite successful in his business. He used that success to provide for his family. Between 1876 and 1886, he purchased three contiguous tracts of land (a total of twelve acres) several miles north of Christiansburg on which he and Eliza lived until they died—Walter sometime between 1900 and 1910 and Eliza in 1920. The couple was especially concerned to care for their two children, Nannie and Robert Cutler, and worked diligently to provide them advantages they had never enjoyed themselves. When Nannie turned six, for example, her parents opened an account for her in the Freedman's Saving and Trust Company, and both Nannie and Cutler were later sent to Shaw University.[40]

A third McNorton brother, Orville, also spent most of his adult life in Montgomery County. Orville had remained at Smithfield in the division of James Patton Preston's estate and in 1863 had married Easter Jane Fraction, who lived at White Thorn with her mother, Virginia Fraction Caperton. Orville and Easter Jane remained together for more than forty years, had at least twelve children, and achieved a significant level of economic and social success.

As a freedman, Orville initially worked for the Virginia and Tennessee Railroad. This was one of the best ways a Black man in Montgomery County could earn cash wages immediately after the Civil War, and Orville used his earnings to become one of the first of those formerly enslaved at Smithfield known to have acquired his own land. Indeed, sometime between 1868 and 1871, McNorton bought part of the very plantation on which he and his family had been enslaved. When the property of William Ballard Preston had finally been divided in 1865, Preston's son, J. Patton Preston, had received 126 acres immediately adjacent to the tract his mother retained as her dower. Within three years, Patton Preston sold part of that land to Thomas Wilson, who then sold four acres of it to Orville McNorton. McNorton did not hold the land for long; in 1871 he sold it to Robert T. Preston and bought from Preston nine acres northwest of Smithfield. Neither McNorton nor Preston recorded how he felt about those transactions, but knowing how Robert T. Preston interacted with other freedpeople, it is tempting to believe that he was incensed at Orville McNorton owning a part of the Preston homeplace and that McNorton was able to drive a hard bargain when he sold it. Eight years later, in 1879, McNorton sold the land he had acquired from Robert T. Preston and bought an even larger piece of the Preston domain. This time he bought 107 acres from the estate of

William Ballard Preston, his former owner. The land lay west of White Thorn and seems never to have been part of Smithfield proper. McNorton resold half of this land within five years but seems to have lived and farmed on the other half for more than a decade. In 1892, he sold or traded the last of his former Preston land and moved closer to his brothers, settling on twenty-five acres just north of Cambria.[41]

Orville McNorton did very well for a Black man in Montgomery County at that time. By 1880 he was one of the leading Black landowners in the county, and the assessed value of his personal property that year placed him among the top 5 percent of African Americans on the county's tax roll. He also participated as much and as skillfully in the political and legal systems of the county as any Black man could at the time. He was one of several hundred who voted in the county between 1867, when freedmen first voted in Virginia, and 1902, when a new state constitution stripped nearly all Black men of the franchise. He was also one of just two dozen African Americans who served on a jury in Montgomery County during those years. For a short time in the early 1880s, a judge in the county began seating mixed-race grand juries. He seems to have chosen only well-respected Black men as jurors, and he selected Orville McNorton to serve twice in 1883. A decade later, McNorton showed just how well he understood the legal system of Virginia. When creditors began pressing him for payment of monies he owed, he sold his land to his wife and children for token amounts, though he retained a life interest in the property. Two of his creditors then brought suit to void one of the sales on the grounds that it was made "with the intent to hinder, delay, and defraud your orator in the collection of his debt," which McNorton later admitted was exactly what he had done. The tactic bought McNorton enough time to pay the debt and avoid losing "his little home," but he later had to sue his own son, Chester, to recover part of his property.[42]

The suit against Chester, brought in 1906, was apparently part of a dispute between Orville and two of his sons about how best to approach his final years. By then, Orville was in his mid-sixties, and his sons Chester and Stanley had been trying for several years to convince him to sell the home place "as we have to look out for you in your old days." Chester and Stanley wanted to sell the property, put the proceeds in a bank, and bring their parents to live with Stanley, who owned a bar and livery stable in Glen Jean, West Virginia. "You will be of good service to him in helping around the stable," Chester had written in 1904; "work or play or what you may do, so take things easy and don't kick until you are spured." Initially, Orville and Easter Jane refused. But in 1906 Frank McNorton, the couple's youngest child and the only one still living in Montgomery County, was killed in a mining accident, and by 1909 Easter Jane had died as well. Finally, in the spring of 1910, Orville relented. He sold his remaining land in Montgomery County and went to live with Stanley and his family in West Virginia. Two years later, Stanley moved the family to New Richmond, Ohio, and Orville moved with them. He died there on August 20, 1916, but was taken back to Virginia for burial.[43]

Orville's brother Robert, the youngest of William and Catherine McNorton's sons, also settled in Montgomery County after his emancipation. Robert had remained at Smithfield when the estate of James Patton Preston was divided and may have escaped slavery along with Thomas and Othello Fraction and other men from Montgomery County who followed Union cavalry out of the county in April 1865. McNorton claimed to have enlisted in the Fortieth United States Colored Infantry, as the Fractions had, but no record has survived to confirm his claim, and his application for a military pension was denied for that reason. If McNorton did serve in the Fortieth USCI, he may have initially remained in Tennessee after the regiment mustered out because there is no evidence of his presence back in Montgomery County until 1869. When he did return, he seems to have apprenticed under his brother Walter and become a carpenter. In the summer of 1869 Walter and Robert built Othello Fraction's house in Salem, and according to the federal census Robert was living with Walter and Eliza in 1870. Within a few years, though, Robert was making his own way in the world. In 1874 he bought a lot in Cambria, just uphill from his brother Taylor, and in 1878 he married Ellen Calloway, with whom he had at least nine children over the next twenty-five years. Robert McNorton died in 1917 and Ellen in 1947.[44]

Eliza McNorton also seems to have been living at White Thorn when slavery ended. Eliza had married a man named Rubin Burke, or Burks, about 1840 and had at least three children with him by 1851. Medical records indicate that Rubin was also enslaved at White Thorn, but his name vanished from the records after 1856, suggesting that he had died, run away, or been sold. Eliza and her children were still at White Thorn in 1862, when they appeared on the probate inventory of James F. Preston, but no record has yet been found to show what Eliza did immediately after gaining her freedom. Post-emancipation records of Eliza are scarce but suggest

During the 1890s, William Poindexter (seated on the right) served as a deacon of Memorial Baptist Church in Christiansburg. (Author's collection)

that she remained in Montgomery County until her death and lived as a dependent of her siblings or children. The first such record, the 1870 federal census, shows her and her daughter, Grace, living in the home of Eliza's sister, Grace McNorton. Ten years later, in 1880, she was living with her daughter Charlotte Burke Smith and Charlotte's family, next door to her brother Walter McNorton, and in 1900 Eliza was living with her daughter, Grace Burks Strother, next door to her brother Taylor. Five years later, in April 1905, Eliza McNorton Burks died and was buried in Christiansburg.[45]

Eliza McNorton Burks's two oldest daughters, Elizabeth and Charlotte, were also adults when freedom came. Elizabeth Burks had married William Poindexter in 1861, when she was just sixteen. Poindexter had been enslaved by William Ballard Preston, though it is not clear if he lived at Smithfield or on one of Preston's Henry County plantations. William Poindexter was also a blacksmith, a skilled trade that may have helped the family make the transition to freedom more easily than some of its peers. Immediately after emancipation, the couple lived at White Thorn, working for

Elizabeth's former owner. By 1870, though, they had moved to Christiansburg and settled there. In his later years, William's heart disease may have restricted the family's material success but not its standing in the community; William served as a deacon of Memorial Baptist Church (known today as Schaeffer Memorial Baptist Church), the most prominent Black church in the county. The couple had no children of their own but seem to have raised several of their nieces and nephews. Following William's death in 1902, Elizabeth married James Taylor, a son of the county's best-known Black minister. After Taylor's death in 1919, she moved to Roanoke to live with a married niece but moved back to Montgomery County when she married Peter Fliggins in 1922. She then remained in the county when Peter died in 1928 and died there herself in 1935. Elizabeth's sister Charlotte Burke had married John Smith in 1863 and already had two children when slavery ended. Initially, her family also lived at White Thorn, working for Sarah Preston, but by 1870 had moved to Christiansburg and was living next door to William and Elizabeth Poindexter. Apparently the Smiths remained in Christiansburg until at least 1890, when they buried their son William there. After that, however, their story has been lost in a sea of Smiths.[46]

Eliza McNorton Burks's youngest daughter, Grace, was fourteen when slavery ended. Like her sisters, she began her life as a freedwoman working for her former owner, Sarah Preston. She then lived briefly with her aunt, Grace McNorton, with whom she and her mother were living in 1870. The following year she married Steward Strother and in the years that followed had at least six children with him. Steward had died or left by 1900. Grace was living with her mother that year and supporting herself as a dressmaker. After her mother's death in 1905, Grace moved to Tazewell County, where she was living with two of her sons in 1910, and by 1920 had gone to live with her son, Rutherford, in Dayton, Ohio. She died there in January 1930.[47]

Grace McNorton, the sister of Eliza McNorton Burks, seems to have been enslaved at Solitude until 1865. Nothing is known of her partner(s) or marital status, though she had at least four children between 1850 and 1860 and later identified herself as a widow. In 1867, she and her children were living in Christiansburg with her brother Walter and his family, and in 1870 she and two of her sons were living with her sister Eliza. Sometime in the next decade, however, she moved to Parkersburg, West Virginia, a transportation hub where two turnpikes and a railroad reached the Ohio River.

There she initially found work as a chambermaid on an Ohio River steamboat and later worked as a housekeeper. She died in Parkersburg in 1907.[48]

Among the generation who moved from slavery at Smithfield to freedom in 1865, the Fractions and Grace McNorton were unusual in their decision to leave the communities they had known so soon after gaining their freedom. Most of those who had been enslaved by the Prestons chose to remain in Montgomery County as freedpeople, while those held by the Gilmers either remained in Pittsylvania County or rejoined their families in Montgomery. Given the lack of material resources with which they began their new lives and their lack of experience in or knowledge of a wider world, this is hardly surprising. An even greater barrier to moving, though, may have been the fact that no one in that wider world knew them or their character. Beyond Montgomery or Pittsylvania Counties no one knew them, and in a world with few reliable methods to verify one's identity and condition, leaving the worlds in which they were known was a bold, even reckless, move—especially for people of color. For poor, newly freed, African Americans it took extraordinary courage or utter desperation to leave the only worlds they had ever known and start again in a community of strangers. Even the Fractions might have remained in Montgomery County but for the confidence Oscar, Thomas, and Othello had gained while serving in the army.

Among the generation that followed, however, this pattern changed dramatically. Some of those born after 1865 remained among the familiar places and people of the communities in which they were born, but many more ventured out into strange new worlds. And those who did so, travelled far and wide and made their marks in a variety of ways.

6

Outward and Upward

I n the decades between the Civil War and the opening of the twentieth
century, families that had once been enslaved at Smithfield continued
to grow. Among the children and grandchildren of William and Catherine McNorton, John and Easther Fraction, Margaret and Richard Saunders, William and Louisa Moon, and Cynthia Franklin were almost one
hundred individuals born between 1850 and 1903. Most of these men and
women were not even born until after slavery had ended, while others born
during slavery came of age only after emancipation. The opportunities available to them were still sharply constrained by the racial attitudes of the day,
but they were far greater than those afforded their parents or grandparents.
To a much greater extent than earlier generations, Black Virginians could
now live where they wanted to and move when they wanted to; they married when they wanted to and who they wanted to; and they made careers
not only as farmers and laborers but also as teachers and professionals.

Among the members of this new generation whose histories can be
reconstructed, about a third remained in Virginia. Most of these stayed in
Montgomery or Pittsylvania Counties, where their parents and grandparents had been enslaved, though some moved elsewhere in the commonwealth. Like many Black Virginians at that time, these men and women
generally worked as servants or manual laborers. Hellis Franklin married
a neighbor, Albert Pigg, and remained a servant at White Thorn; her son,
Nathaniel, worked as a teamster in Blacksburg. Edward Patton McNorton also worked as a teamster, and Ballard McNorton was a hostler. Flynt
McNorton, Mansel Moon, and Daniel Moon were laborers, and William

Moon was a farm laborer. Laura Saunders was a laundress, and Sarah Capers and Amanda Saunders were servants. Not all worked as servants or laborers, though. Lillie McNorton served as a teacher before marrying her cousin Chester and leaving for Montana; her sister, Lizzie, married Hugh Campbell, a Christiansburg carpenter. Victor Moon owned his own farm in Campbell County, and in Pittsylvania County Frank McNorton's son, Montreville, worked as a carpenter while two of his daughters, Emily and Catherine, became public school teachers. Frank McNorton's youngest daughter, Elizabeth, worked as a dressmaker and lived in next-door Halifax County with her husband, a farmer.[1]

Staying in Virginia was not easy, though. Members of the post-emancipation generation certainly experienced greater freedom than Black Virginians had enjoyed before 1865. Laws restricting their movement, excluding them from certain occupations, and criminalizing any effort to educate them had all been abolished, and African Americans in Montgomery County had taken advantage of these new opportunities to establish a close-knit community in which members supported one another in a variety of ways. The modest economic success of their parents after emancipation also meant that members of the postwar generation were often better equipped financially to make their own way in the world. Members of this new generation, however, still faced both racism and economic challenges in Virginia long after the abolition of slavery. Indeed, the racial and economic challenges facing African Americans grew in Virginia at the dawn of the twentieth century.

Like other states in the former Confederacy, Virginia had reluctantly accepted the need to grant African American men the right to vote as the price of rejoining the Union. As a result, between 1867 and 1902, Black men across the commonwealth often voted and in some communities were elected to office. During these years, Virginia saw Black local officials, Black members of the General Assembly, and one Black member of Congress. Social relations between the races were still strained during these years, interracial marriage was illegal, and public schools were racially segregated, but the extensive and degrading range of restrictions known as Jim Crow had not yet begun. During the final years of the nineteenth century, however, White Virginians became increasingly dissatisfied with even the limited rights and privileges enjoyed by Black Virginians, and in 1902 they called a state convention to draft a new constitution that virtually eliminated Black voting in Virginia and set the stage for the Jim Crow era in Virginia. The

United States Supreme Court had recently gutted the Fourteenth Amendment and ruled that separate but equal racial segregation was constitutional. Now, with few Black voters to object and the blessing of federal courts, local and state officials in Virginia began to adopt greater restrictions on where and how Blacks could live, work, and travel in the commonwealth.[2]

In addition to growing racial discrimination, the children of people who had been enslaved at Smithfield often faced increased economic challenges as they came of age. Farmworkers across Virginia suffered along with the rest of the agricultural economy through an era of low prices and increased competition, and many Black workers found themselves trapped in debt and exploitive sharecropping agreements. Sharecropping never became a major element of the economy in Montgomery County, and a significant number of Black families acquired land of their own in the decades following emancipation. Their holdings, however, often consisted of rocky, hilly land on which commercial farming was extremely difficult. They were also relatively small tracts, which made it difficult for fathers to provide their children with acreage enough to make a living. Nor were there many non-agricultural options available to Black Virginians. New industries appeared in Virginia and older ones continued to expand, but the jobs they created seldom went to African Americans. Railroads hired Black men, especially for track maintenance, and tobacco factories often relied on Black workers for more onerous tasks, such stripping stems from the leaves, but most other industrial work in Virginia was generally reserved for White workers.[3]

In the face of such challenges, some Black Virginians left temporarily in order to gain skills or experience that would permit them to lead better lives back in Virginia. This was the path chosen by Walter McNorton's son, Robert Cutler. Born in 1874, Cutler grew up in Christiansburg, where his father was a carpenter and a respected member of the county's Black community. Cutler received his early education at the Christiansburg Institute, southwest Virginia's premier educational institution for African Americans, and set his sights on a medical career. His interest in medicine may have been influenced by his brother-in-law, Robert A. Reynolds. Reynolds, who married Cutler's sister Nannie in 1888, was a physician in Danville, Virginia, and a graduate of Leonard Medical School. Leonard Medical School was part of Shaw University, in Raleigh, North Carolina, and at the time was one of a handful of institutions in the United States training Black physicians. When Cutler expressed an interest in medicine, Dr. Reynolds suggested that he consider Shaw University, which he did. By 1891, Cutler was enrolled at Shaw as an undergraduate studying pharmacy, and in 1894 he graduated from the Leonard School of Pharmacy. He had done well in college, and hoped to establish himself in Danville, but the Virginia medical board refused to certify him. Instead, he moved to Americus, Georgia, to work in a pharmacy operated by E. H. Brinson. In the summer of 1898, however, he returned Virginia and enlisted as a hospital steward in the Sixth Virginia Volunteer Infantry.[4]

Four months earlier, in April 1898, the United States had declared war on Spain and launched the Spanish American War. Many African Americans were eager to join the war effort and to demonstrate both their patriotism and the fact that they were just as capable of military service as White men were. Their options were limited, though. The regular army included just four Black regiments, all stationed in the West, and few White Americans were enthusiastic about creating new ones. Several states, however, already had Black militia units that could be called up to help meet their quotas when President McKinley called for volunteers. Among these states was Virginia, which had two battalions of "colored infantry" in its state militia. These became the core of the Sixth Virginia Infantry, and Cutler McNorton was one of many Black Virginians who enlisted in the regiment during the summer of 1898 as recruiters raised its strength and it entered federal service.[5]

The Sixth Virginia Infantry never made it to Cuba. After initial training outside Richmond, it underwent additional training at Camp Poland in Tennessee. During the months at Camp Poland, already strained relations between the regiment's White commander and its Black company and battalion officers faced even greater strain. The situation came to a head when the White colonel commanding the Sixth convened a review board to evaluate the qualifications of its Black officers. In protest, nine Black officers resigned, and over strenuous protests from the regiment and from the Black press, the officers were replaced by White officers. Initially, rank-and-file members of the regiment refused to obey any orders from their new White officers, and the "mutiny" was only ended through the efforts of the remaining Black officers. Shortly afterwards, the Sixth Virginia was sent to Camp Haskell, outside Macon, Georgia, and discipline deteriorated even further. Racial segregation was more obvious and more virulent in Georgia than it was in Virginia at that time, and soldiers from the Sixth Virginia often refused to tolerate the blatant discrimination they encountered in

Macon. White officers, however, had no sympathy for such behavior, and when armed Black soldiers attempted to enter White-only bars and restaurants in Macon, the entire regiment was disarmed, arrested, and confined to camp. Six weeks later, in January 1899, the Sixth Virginia was mustered out and sent back to Richmond.[6]

For Cutler McNorton, service in "the mutinous Sixth" did have a silver lining. During the regiment's brief stay in Georgia, he met and married Lou Ella Slaton. The couple wed in December 1898, and Lou Ella moved to Virginia when Cutler mustered out. Nor did Cutler's experience in the Sixth Virginia deter him from reenlisting shortly after returning to Virginia. In July 1899, he enlisted for three years and was made a hospital steward in the Forty-Ninth United States Volunteer Infantry, a new Black regiment raised that summer for service in the Philippines. Once again, though, Cutler's military service was cut short. Either he was injured soon after enlisting or an earlier injury reappeared. He was discharged just two months after enlisting without ever leaving the United States and spent the rest of his life as an invalid on a military pension living in Christiansburg. He died there in 1932. Lou Ella also remained in Christiansburg until her death in 1953. She enjoyed a long career as teacher at Cutler's alma mater, the Christiansburg Institute, where the couple's only child, Cutler Reynolds McNorton, also studied before attending the Hampton Institute and embarking on a career in insurance.[7]

Unlike Cutler McNorton, many other descendants of families enslaved at Smithfield responded to the rising racial and economic pressure in Virginia by leaving the commonwealth for good. Among the generation of those who were still children when slavery ended or were born after emancipation, dozens left Virginia permanently when they came of age. No one motive explains their decision to emigrate, and no single destination attracted them all, but family often played an important role both in deciding to leave Virginia and in picking a place to go. Descendants of the men and women enslaved at Smithfield often demonstrated what is sometimes called chain migration. One family member led the way to a particular destination, and his or her success there convinced others to follow. Success also made it possible for those who went first to provide critical support to those who came after them. This pattern was evident repeatedly among the Fraction, Moon, and McNorton families well into the twentieth century.

For those leaving Virginia in the closing decades of the nineteenth century, one of the most attractive destinations was West Virginia. These decades saw a massive expansion of coal mining in West Virginia, and unlike most of the mines in southwestern Virginia, those in West Virginia were often willing to hire Black men. This created a range of new opportunities for Black workers in the mines and in industries supported by mining and miners. Not only did many of these jobs pay better than those available to Blacks in Virginia but also West Virginia was relatively close to home, making it easier for those who migrated to keep in touch with parents and siblings left behind. By the 1880s Black Virginians had already begun moving to the coal mining districts of West Virginia, and their number increased steadily over the next several decades.[8]

Many of those who moved were men seeking jobs in the mines, on the railroads that moved the coal, in other industries supported by mining, and in those serving the growing African American community. Wilson Capers moved to West Virginia sometime between 1880 and 1900 and settled in Fayette County, where he worked as a laborer and then a railroad yardman. His brother Jasper settled in Kanawah County and began working in the Hotel Ruffner but ended up in the county poorhouse. Ballard McNorton, a son of Orville, moved to Bluefield early in the twentieth century and worked for forty years as a brakeman on the Norfolk & Western Railway. Chloe Fraction's son, Samuel Shorts Jr., had moved to West Virginia by 1891 and went to work as a coke puller in Mercer County. Saunders Moon Jr., graduated from Virginia Normal and Collegiate Institute in 1898 and began teaching in Pittsylvania County, Virginia, but early in the twentieth century he moved to McDowell County, West Virginia. There he married Mattie Froe in 1907 and had at least eight children before his death in 1929. Saunders may still have worked as a teacher, but the 1910 census identified him as a lawyer, and the obituary of his daughter, Olga, described him as an attorney.[9]

Daughters of those enslaved at Smithfield also moved to West Virginia. Some did so on their own to work in industries surrounding the mining economy, but most seem to have gone as the wives of men who did so. Mary Kate McNorton, Taylor McNorton's daughter, moved to Parkersburg, where her husband, James Porter, found work as a miner. Both of Orville McNorton's daughters, Ethel and Florence, also married West Virginia miners. Ethel seems to have moved to West Virginia from New Jersey following the death of her first husband, Robert Hughes, and may have done so because her brother, Stanley, had already settled in Fayette County. There she married Robert Peters in 1894 and raised two daughters, Ada

Ethel and Ada Peters, daughters of Florence McNorton Peters, published *War Poems* in 1919 "to show the Negro's loyalty to the Stars and Stripes, in the war with Germany; and to show the need of unity in all men in the fight for democracy." (West Virginia State Archives)

and Ethel, who as teenagers published *War Poems,* a book of poetry honoring Black soldiers during World War I. Florence McNorton, also came to Fayette County, where she married Jacob Price in 1895. Her new life was tragically brief, though. Just a year after her wedding she bled to death following the birth of her son, Jacob Jr. Delphia Moon, the daughter of Preston Moon, married William Woodson in 1897, but the couple seems to have had trouble establishing themselves in Virginia. Soon after the turn of the century they moved to Mercer County, West Virginia, where William began a career in coal mining.[10]

Among the children who migrated to West Virginia, the most successful may have been Stanley McNorton, the second son of Orville McNorton. Born in Montgomery County about 1870, Stanley moved to Fayette County, West Virginia, in his late teens or early twenties and by 1894 had settled in the booming coal town of Glen Jean. There he married Emma Harris, also an immigrant from Virginia, and began raising a family. Like thousands of other young men in the region, Stanley began working as a coal miner. By 1900, though, he had escaped the mines and over the next decade became a "prominent colored business man" engaged in multiple activities. Initially, he catered to the miners' thirst for alcohol and excitement, operating the Ape Yard Saloon and the Coney Island Saloon, both of which were known for their rowdy atmosphere. By 1908 he had moved into the livery business with a stock of horses, mules, buggies, wagons, saddles, and lap robes available for purchase or hire. He also provided draft animals to some of the coal mines in and around Glen Jean, travelling as far as Kansas City and Fort Worth to purchase mining mules that he shipped by rail to West Virginia.[11]

As he prospered economically, Stanley McNorton also reached out to help his family and his community. He supported both his brother, Chester, and his brother-in-law, Jacob Price, when they needed help getting back on their feet, and brought his father to live with him in Glen Jean following the death of his mother. He also supported Fayette County's African American community. In 1908, fire destroyed most of the West Virginia Industrial School, Seminary, and College, which Baptists had established to train Black teachers. When local residents mobilized to rebuild it, McNorton "came with his teams and a force of men . . . [who] began the work with a will." And he was active in local Republican politics, running for local office and serving, as one scholar wrote, "[in] the vanguard of West Virginia's Black political leaders."[12]

By 1912, Glen Jean was still booming, but early that year Stanley decided— or was forced—to sell out and move to Ohio. In 1910 and 1911, he and Emma had borrowed against real estate they owned and the stock of the livery stable. By early 1912 they had repaid at least some of the money they owed, but in January they sold the stock of the livery stable, perhaps to settle the remainder of their debt. Then, or soon after, Stanley, Emma, their three children, and Stanley's father moved to Ohio and settled in New Richmond, a small Ohio River town twenty-five miles from Cincinnati. Stanley went into farming, initially, but by 1920 was working in Cincinnati as a labor agent for a coal company. He remained in Cincinnati until his death in 1937, working for several employment agencies before opening one of his own. He also remained active in efforts to improve conditions for African Americans. In 1920, John Whitelaw Lewis, a businessman and activist in Washington, DC, invited "some of the leading colored businessmen in the several states" to a meeting at which Lewis proposed the creation of a "national commercial enterprise that will be a benefit to the colored people in the United States." Out of this meeting came the National Mutual Improvement Association of America with Stanley McNorton as its vice president.[13]

West Virginia was by no means the only destination to which the descendants of those enslaved at Smithfield migrated at the close of the nineteenth century. As described in the preceding chapter, members of the Fraction family had begun moving to Maryland in the 1870s. That migration continued through the 1890s, and by the early twentieth century Baltimore had become the family's new center. Othello Fraction had moved to Baltimore during the 1870s and lived there until his death in 1904. Othello's son, Roosevelt, died in 1909 at age seven, but his daughter, Eva, married and had at least four children, whose descendants still live in the Baltimore area. Thomas Fraction, Othello's brother, never moved north, remaining in Salem until his death in 1892. His widow, Isabella, and three of the couple's children, however, also moved to Baltimore. His daughter Mary Ellen, born in 1871, went first; by 1893 she was living in Baltimore and married to Thomas Diggs. It is unclear whether Mary Ellen moved to Baltimore and met Diggs there or married him elsewhere and then moved, but once married the couple made their home in Baltimore and had at least four children between 1893 and 1899. Thomas worked as a laborer until his death between 1910 and 1920. Mary Ellen then supported herself as a laundress and servant and maintained her own household for another twenty years. By 1940, though, she had moved in with her son Frank and his family and lived with them until her death in 1946. Mary Ellen's younger brothers, John and Frank, seem to have moved to Baltimore with their mother shortly after their father died. John, born in 1877, barely had time to settle in the city before he was killed in a shooting accident early in 1897. Isabella Fraction and ten-year-old Frank initially lived with Mary Ellen and Thomas Diggs when they moved to Baltimore, and Isabella spent the rest of her life with Mary Ellen's family. Frank lived with the Diggs until 1906, when he married Blanche Henson. He and Blanche had at least two children during the next five years, but Blanche died about 1913, and the family separated. The children were sent to an orphanage in Baltimore, and Frank began living as a lodger. Frank continued to work as a laborer and live as a lodger until his death in 1949. His children eventually established families of their own and their descendants remain in Baltimore today.[14]

Cynthia Franklin's daughter Henrietta also left Virginia during the 1880s, but she went west. Henrietta Franklin was born into slavery at White Thorn in 1854, gained her freedom as a child, and came of age in post-Reconstruction

Montgomery County. She married David Hickman, a farmworker, in 1874, but early in the 1880s the family moved to Perry County, Ohio, probably to Rendville. Perry County was part of Ohio's Appalachian coal mining district and home to an expanding number of mining towns. Among those towns, Rendville was unique. When it was established in 1879, its founder broke with local practice and began hiring Black miners. This brought a number of Black Virginians to Rendville, including the Hickmans. The family stayed in Perry County for just a few years, though, and by 1885 had moved on to Mahaska County, Iowa, where Black workers had recently been recruited to break a strike by White coal miners in the county. Over the next two decades, the Hickmans moved from town to town in southern Iowa as coal mines opened and closed in the region. They eventually settled in Buxton, the largest and most prosperous of Iowa's African American mining communities, and their children became miners or married miners.[15]

The extent and nature of the exodus that occurred at the close of the nineteenth century was especially evident among the McNortons. The founders of the family, William and Catherine McNorton, spent their entire adult lives enslaved at Smithfield and died there between 1862 and 1865. They had at least thirteen children while held by the Prestons, and when slavery ended at least eight of them were still being held in Montgomery or Pittsylvania County; their son Ballard had died at White Thorn in 1862, and four other children had either died or been sold. Of the eight who were emancipated in 1865, only Grace left Virginia to start a new life, settling with her children in Parkersburg, West Virginia. The next generation, however, was much more footloose. The seven children of William and Catherine McNorton who stayed in Virginia had thirty-five children, and twenty-four of them left the commonwealth when they came of age. As described above, some of William and Catherine's grandchildren settled in West Virginia or southern Ohio. Others, however, went much farther afield.

William and Catherine's oldest son, Taylor, had four children who lived to be adults, and two of them left Virginia for Texas. Hugh Fleming McNorton was born at White Thorn in 1859 and grew up near Christiansburg, where his father worked as a farmhand and owned a small house lot. In the late 1870s or early 1880s Fleming attended the Wayland Seminary, a Baptist institution with branches in Richmond and Washington, DC. He then became a Baptist minister, which may be what took him to

Texas. By 1884 he had settled in Red River County, where he soon met Laura Bowers, the daughter of a local farmer. The couple married in 1885, moved to Clarksville, the county seat, and began to establish a very successful life together. Fleming served both as preacher in the Baptist church and as a teacher in the segregated public school system. Laura opened a millinery and dressmaking shop and operated a school of dressmaking. The couple remained in Clarksville for almost thirty years and had five daughters between 1886 and 1901. In 1914, though, the family moved to Fort Worth. There Fleming continued preaching and teaching and at least four of the couple's daughters married. They, in turn, continued to move. Serena and her husband, James Jackson, moved to Los Angeles shortly after the First World War. Three others—Geneva, Corrine, and Carrie—married railroad postal clerks and with their husbands all moved north to Cincinnati around 1930. Fleming and Laura soon followed, and both died in Cincinnati in 1935.[16]

Fleming McNorton's younger brother, Charles, seems to have followed Fleming to Texas. Born at White Thorn about 1863, Charles lived with his parents until the mid-1880s. He then attended Shaw University during the 1886–87 school year before moving to Clarksville, Texas, where Fleming and Laura were living. He returned to Shaw for the 1889–90 and 1891–92 terms but does not seem to have graduated. By 1895 he had returned to Texas and settled in Dallas. There he found work as a coachman and began courting a young woman named Sadie Johnson. The courtship, however, went horribly awry. Newspaper accounts report that Charles and Sadie "were standing before a minister in the church . . . about to be married" when Sadie "refused to have the ceremony performed." Enraged by her refusal, McNorton reportedly cried "death or marriage" and shot his reluctant bride. Sadie Johnson died, and Charles McNorton was convicted of "assault to murder." He was sentenced to five years in a state prison but was pardoned after two, and by 1900 he was working as a waiter in Dallas. Three years later he married Lena Heflin in Palestine, Texas, and by 1909 the couple had moved to California with their daughter, Mamie, and Lena's widowed mother. There they had a son, Taylor, and Charles found work as a cook. In 1910 he was cooking at a hotel in San Diego and by 1920 was the chef on a railroad dining car. By then the family had moved to Los Angeles, where Charles died in 1926. Taylor, his son, had died several years earlier, but Lena and Mamie remained in Los Angeles, where Lena died in 1965.[17]

William and Catherine McNorton's son Frank had been taken to the Gilmer plantation in Pittsylvania County when the estate of James Patton Preston was divided, and after emancipation he remained in that county until his death. The paths followed by his children are unclear, but at least two of the eight left Virginia. His daughter Harriet married Stephen Woods, a local man, in 1898 and moved with him almost immediately afterwards to Winston-Salem, North Carolina. Winston-Salem was the home of R. J. Reynolds tobacco, and Stephen spent the next thirty years working in tobacco factories there. Harriet, or Hattie, raised the couple's four children and for a time operated a boardinghouse. She died in 1931. Her brother James went north as an adult, though when and how he did so remain a mystery. He was born in Pittsylvania County in 1878, but by 1917 was married, working as a machinist, and living in New York City. He seems to have stayed in New York until his death, sometime after 1940, and had at least one child.[18]

The most widely scattered of William and Catherine McNorton's grandchildren were those of their son Orville and his wife, Easter Jane Fraction. Orville and Easter Jane had married in 1863 and had twelve children over the next thirty years. The youngest of these, Frank, died in Montgomery County as teenager, but by then all his of siblings had already moved out of Virginia. As described above, four of them—Ethel, Florence, Stanley, and Ballard—settled in the coalfields of West Virginia, though Stanley eventually moved to southern Ohio. The other children of Orville and Easter Jane, all boys, chose very different paths.

Minor McNorton seems to have followed the railroad out of Virginia. Born in 1881, Minor lived at home with his parents until 1900, at least. By 1910, he had made his way to Madison County, Tennessee, where he married Dorothy Weaver. Unfortunately, the record of their marriage provides neither Minor's residence nor his occupation. By 1915, though, he was employed as a railroad brakeman, and by 1918 he and Dorothy had settled in Chattanooga. Minor continued to work for the Southern Railway until at least 1942 and the couple remained in Chattanooga until their deaths—hers in 1972 and his in 1975. They had no children of their own but adopted a great-nephew, Simon, and raised him as their son.[19]

Augustine Joseph Orville McNorton, known both as Orville Jr. and as Augustine, also spent time in Tennessee but for very different reasons. Born in 1880, Orville spent his childhood in Christiansburg and probably began his education at the Christiansburg Institute. He then went on to attend the

Richmond Theological Institute and was enrolled there in 1899 when the school merged with Wayland Seminary to form Virginia Union University. Two years later, in May 1901, he was one of four graduates from the new university's Academic Department. Following his graduation, Orville seems to have spent time with his brother, Stanley, in Glen Jean, West Virginia, and was living there in 1902 when he filed for two United States patents. In August 1902, Orville McNorton Jr. submitted patent applications for an improved automatic railroad switch and for a music holder and turner for use on pianos, and both patents were granted the following year. By then Orville had moved to Baltimore and begun working as a teacher and a stenographer. He had also he left the Baptist faith in which he had been raised and converted to Catholicism, which he described as "our only hope as a race." Inspired to become a priest, Augustine, as he now called himself, enrolled at St. Joseph's Seminary, one of the few Catholic seminaries in the United States open to African Americans, but left without completing his studies. Instead, he joined forces with a prominent Black publisher, Edward E. Cooper, to start a newspaper. Cooper had previously published the *Indianapolis Freeman* and the *Colored American*. Now, with support from James Cardinal Gibbons, the Archbishop of Baltimore, he and McNorton established the *Colored Catholic Herald*, a weekly publication featuring material "pertaining to the colored people in general as they relate to the Catholic faith."[20]

The *Colored Catholic Herald* did not last long. It is unclear precisely when it ceased operations, but the paper certainly lasted no more than a few years. When it folded, Augustine McNorton vanished from the historical record until he and his wife, Mary, appeared in Nashville, Tennessee, in 1914. No record has yet surfaced to show who Mary was or when the couple married. By 1914, though, Augustine had undergone yet another transformation. Not only had he married, he had enrolled in medical school. He was in Nashville attending Meharry Medical College, from which he received his degree in 1916. He and Mary then moved to Chicago, settled in "Bronzeville"—the heart of Chicago's African American community—and began raising two daughters, Mary and Eloise, while Augustine established himself as a physician. The life they created in Chicago, however, proved short-lived. Mary McNorton died in 1926. Augustine may then have moved to Lucas County, Ohio, where his brother Burman was living, or may have simply been visiting there when he died of a ruptured appendix in 1929.[21]

Of all the paths followed out of Virginia by Orville McNorton's children, none was more adventurous than that first blazed by William McNorton and subsequently followed by four of his brothers: Chester, Walter, Burman, and Hugh. Between 1885 and 1910, five sons of Orville McNorton and Easter Jane Fraction McNorton left their home outside of Christiansburg and moved to Montana.

William McNorton was born in 1867. He was Orville and Easter Jane's eldest son and as boy worked on the farm his parents had established soon after their emancipation. By the time he turned twenty, though, William had moved to Montana. Unfortunately, it is impossible to say how or why he decided to move there. Montana was not yet even a state in 1887; its non–Native American population was less than 130,000; and fewer than 1,500 of those were Black. A newspaper article about McNorton written in the 1930s reported that he had come to Montana in 1887 and that "he recounted to his friends . . . that he had left Virginia and sought his fortune in the west so that he would not be restricted from opportunity by racial prejudices as he would be in the south." Neither the date of his arrival nor the reason for his move can be confirmed from other sources, but the paper's report seems reasonable. McNorton was certainly in Montana by the early 1890s, and while White Montanans were hardly blind to his race (in later years he was often described in the local press as "Nigger Bill") surviving evidence suggests that he was well-respected by many of his neighbors.[22]

William McNorton's western adventure may have begun in Butte. The Anaconda Copper Mine opened there in 1881, and within ten years the town had a large enough African American population to support a congregation of the African Methodist Episcopal Church. In June 1887, a local newspaper reported that William McNorton had been charged with petty larceny in Butte. There was no mention of this McNorton's race, but Orville's son is the only William McNorton known to have been in Montana at the close of the nineteenth century. If it was him, he did not remain long in Butte as later reports claimed that he had settled near Thompson Falls that same year. Whatever the exact date of his arrival, it must have been fairly soon after 1887, because by 1895, he was already known well enough in Thompson Falls for the local paper to describe him as "one of our best ranchers." Under the Homestead Act, William McNorton eventually gained title to 160 acres in an area called the Blue Slide, some twelve miles west of Thompson Falls, and for two decades he operated what the

Sanders County Ledger called "one of the best ranches hereabouts." He was also active in timber and mining ventures, owned a number of lots in Thompson Falls, and according to newspaper accounts written late in his life was "important and influential and was considered one of the largest taxpayers in the county during the early history of the county."[23]

He was much less successful in his personal life. He married for the first time on July 4, 1900. By the time McNorton died in 1938, this wedding was surrounded by legend, and it is impossible to be certain how much of the story is true. His bride, Ella Horra or Harris, was a White woman from Ohio with a young daughter by as previous marriage. Later accounts described her as a "mail-order bride" who did not know that her husband-to-be was Black. Accounts recorded many years later claimed that Ella did not learn the truth until after her wedding because she arrived in Thompson Falls at sundown and was rushed into a midnight ceremony during which the flickering lamplight made it impossible to judge the groom's race. The story became legendary in Thompson Falls, and it may contain an element of truth: William McNorton was described as very light skinned, and Ella seems not to have known his race until she arrived in Montana. But it seems unlikely that she remained ignorant of the truth until after she said "I do." The couple obtained their marriage license a week before the wedding, and the only known contemporary account of the event says nothing about her being rushed from the train to the alter, only that Ella was "the lady of his choice." However she entered the union, though, Ella soon grew unhappy with her marriage and reportedly "saved nickels and dimes to raise enough money to get a divorce." By May of 1906 she had saved enough, but rather than go to court, she simply moved out. Six months later, her abandoned husband sued for, and obtained, a divorce.[24]

Two years later William tried again. He returned to Virginia in the fall of 1908 to visit his parents and search for another wife. It is unclear whether or not he had a particular woman in mind when he left Montana, but in January 1909 he married India Campbell in Montgomery County. India was, McNorton wrote, "the sweetest and whitest little colored girl I ever saw." She was also just fourteen years old and had spent many of those years living with her widowed grandmother, America Penn, after she and her siblings had been abandoned by their mother. Shortly after their wedding, the newlyweds returned to Thompson Falls, accompanied, or followed soon

William McNorton. (Collection of the Sanders County Historical Society)

after, by India's grandmother, her older brother, Swanson, and William's younger brother, Hugh. This marriage proved even less successful than the first. Eighteen months after her wedding, India McNorton was accused of committing adultery with two different men, both miners boarding at the McNortons' ranch, and of plotting to murder her husband. For her part, India accused William of cruel and inhuman treatment, including repeated physical abuse, and sued for divorce in October 1910. Six months later, the divorce was granted, and William was ordered to pay India $400 plus court costs, though not the permanent alimony she was seeking. In a final bizarre twist to the story, America Penn then went to court and secured a guardian for India on the grounds that she was still a minor, was associating with lewd and dissolute people, and was living a life of idleness, vagrancy, and incorrigibility. It is unclear what happened to India after that, but her grandmother remained William's housekeeper until her death in 1916.[25]

Adding to the turmoil that William McNorton faced in his personal life were several financial setbacks that struck just as his second marriage was unravelling. Shortly before India sued for divorce, William sold his ranch for what the local paper called a "bargain" price, but that was only one of his assets. Three years earlier McNorton had sold two hundred acres of mineral land to a mining company in exchange for stock in what became the Montana Mammoth Mine. With three hundred thousand shares in a mine reported to have "good values in lead and copper and smaller values in silver and gold," McNorton should have been financially secure, but shortly after his second marriage ended, the director of the mining company was convicted in federal court of "using the United States mails in furthering certain worthless mining properties"—including those of the Montana Mammoth Mine. McNorton's three hundred thousand shares seem to have lost their value overnight. He then mortgaged nine town lots he owned in Thompson Falls but fell behind in his payments and lost the lots when the bank foreclosed in 1920. During these years McNorton also secured two patents for improved rail clamps and rail fasteners. The local newspaper reported that he received "many letters from manufacturers" interested in licensing the devices, and rumors circulated that a railroad company had paid $50,000 for them, but if he did receive any money for his inventions it vanished quickly.[26]

It seems likely that the personal and financial difficulties William McNorton encountered also affected his mental health. Writing as "King David," he explained in a letter to the local paper that "Jesus my God . . . came into my house the night of April 13th, 1913 [and] prepared me to tell this world all things are true." For the next twenty-five years, McNorton styled himself as King David and gained a reputation around Thompson Falls as "a religious fanatic." He preached "fire and brimstone" to all who would listen (and to many who preferred not to), described "having trances and seeing visions," and often predicted the end of the world. He also developed an extraordinary garden, vineyard, and orchard on what he called "the Hill of Lord." The site was near his former ranch on property that belonged to a mining company that tolerated him squatting on its land. He raised there a remarkable assortment of fruits and vegetables and often invited the public to share the bounty. At times during these years he wore a crown of thorns around his hat, and from 1926 to 1933 he remained speechless. His silence, he said, was "a punishment placed upon him by the Lord," and he regained his speech only because "the Lord wished to speak to the world." When McNorton did resume speaking, he became increasingly "argumentative," and in May 1938 county officials declared him "dangerous to person and property" and committed him to the state asylum at Warm Springs. Two months later, he died there.[27]

To be sure, William McNorton's story ended badly. But it had started well; for twenty years he enjoyed impressive economic success—especially for a Black man at the dawn of the twentieth century. He was one of the wealthiest men in his community. His real estate holdings included town lots, ranch land, and mining claims and provided him significant profits from ranching and logging. Before his life began its long downward spiral, William McNorton was quite successful, and that success contributed to four of his younger brothers following him west. Between 1890 and 1910, four of McNorton's brothers came to Montana in search of the economic success he enjoyed during those years. The first to do so was Chester.

Born in 1871, Chester McNorton was four years younger than William. Like William, he appeared on the 1880 census living with their parents on the family farm, and like William, he left Montgomery County sometime during the 1880s. By 1890 he was in Evansville, in far southern Indiana. During the final decades of the nineteenth century coalmining expanded significantly in and around Evansville, and Chester may have gone to the region looking for work. If so, he found it, but not as a miner. Instead, he enlisted in the army. During the final years of the Civil War, thousands of Black men had served in the Union army, including three of Chester's great-uncles. After the war, as the army was reorganized and reduced in size, the separate regiments designated United States Colored Troops had been eliminated, but Congress did retain a handful of regiments in the regular army in which African Americans could serve. When this process of reduction and reorganization was finally complete in 1869, the army included four such regiments: Ninth Cavalry, Tenth Cavalry, Twenty-Fourth Infantry, and Twenty-Fifth Infantry. Their commissioned officers were White, but the enlisted men and noncommissioned officers were African American. Reportedly, Native Americans called Black cavalrymen they encountered during the 1870s "buffalo soldiers" because their hair resembled that of a buffalo, and the name soon spread to all four of the army's Black regiments.[28]

In November 1890, Chester McNorton became a buffalo soldier and spent most of the next 13 years in the army. Reenlisting four times and never staying out of the service for more than a couple months, he served almost continuously from November 1890 until July 1903.[29] He was initially assigned to Company F of the Twenty-Fifth Infantry. Elements of the regiment were then stationed at a number of posts across the northern Great Plains, and Company F was based at Fort Missoula, in western Montana. McNorton joined the company in June 1891, four months after it returned to Missoula following its participation in the Pine Ridge Campaign. That turned out to be the army's final campaign against the Plains Indians, and McNorton's company was not one of those used against striking miners in 1892 or to guard railroad property during the railroad strike of 1894. As a result, Chester's early years in the army were fairly routine. He remained a member of the Twenty-Fifth Infantry but changed companies several times and spent time at two other western posts—Fort Assinniboine, in north central Montana, and Fort Buford, on the Montana-North Dakota border. His days were spent, as a history of the regiment put it, "engaged in various duties pertaining to instruction in the art of war." These included drilling and marching, standing guard, digging rifle pits, and manufacturing gabions and fascines. He also enjoyed time away from military routine. He received several furloughs during these years, including an 1891 leave that he spent in Thompson Falls, presumably visiting his brother William.[30]

Chester McNorton was also serving at Fort Missoula when members of his regiment experimented with the military value of bicycles, though he was not part of the experiment himself. In the spring of 1896, Lieutenant James Moss received permission to create the Twenty-Fifth Infantry Bicycle Corps and test the utility of bicycles as military vehicles. Over the next eighteen months, Moss selected two dozen men and tested both men and machines in a series of exercises and rides. Members of the Bicycle Corps regularly rode up to forty miles a day on what passed for roads in Montana carrying their rifles, knapsacks, blankets, and tents with them. They forded streams and practiced getting themselves, their bicycles, and all of their gear over fences up to nine feet tall. In the summer of 1896 they rode eight hundred miles from Missoula to Yellowstone National Park and back and in 1897 followed that expedition with a tortuous journey of nineteen hundred miles from Missoula to Saint Louis. Ultimately, nothing came of the experiment. As Lt. Moss wrote: "The extent of our country, its lack of network roads, its large supply of horses—all these were factors discouraging cycle corps."[31]

Routine army life ended for Chester during his third and fourth tours of duty. In the spring of 1898, he was well into his third tour with the

Twenty-Fifth Infantry and serving at Fort Missoula as a sergeant in Company D. Tension between the United States and Spain had been rising since February, when an explosion sank USS *Maine* in Havana harbor. As talk of war escalated, military planners knew that if fighting did break out the army would need every trained soldier it had, so even before Congress declared war the buffalo soldiers began heading east. Preparations for the move began in late March, and early in April members of the Twenty-Fifth Infantry boarded trains in Montana bound for Florida. From their scattered western posts, the regiment's different companies eventually came together in Tampa, and on June 14 they set sail for Cuba. After eight days in segregated quarters that one Black soldier called "the dirtiest, closest, most sickening place imaginable," the men came ashore in eastern Cuba and joined the American expeditionary force preparing to attack Spanish troops around Santiago de Cuba. When the attack came, on July 1, the Twenty-Fifth Infantry helped to capture enemy fortifications at El Caney in support of the larger and more famous assault on San Juan Hill, in which the three other regiments of buffalo soldiers played conspicuous roles. In both assaults, observers noted that Black soldiers were just as brave and just as effective as their White counterparts. One White correspondent, for example, wrote after the battle: "the services of no four White regiments can be compared with those rendered by the four colored regiments." After several more days of skirmishing, Spanish forces in Santiago agreed to a truce and formally surrendered on July 17. The Twenty-Fifth Infantry then went into camp for several weeks—fighting malaria, typhoid, and dysentery—before returning to the United States in mid-August.[32]

Following its service in Cuba, the Twenty-Fifth Infantry returned to the western United States, but this time to the Department of the Colorado, and Chester McNorton was stationed at Fort Logan, just outside of Denver, as First Sergeant of Company I. Two months after arriving in Colorado, McNorton's enlistment ran out, but he reenlisted immediately and, as a result, was still with the regiment when it shipped out to the Philippines in June 1899. American forces had captured Manila during the Spanish-American War, and under the treaty ending that war Spain had ceded to the United States its colonies in both the Caribbean and the Pacific, including the Philippines. Filipinos, however, had been challenging Spanish control for several years before the Spanish-American War. Indeed, they had declared their independence two months before the war ended, and leaders of the new republic refused to acknowledge the islands' transfer to American control. With American and Filipino troops jostling for control of the region around Manila, it was only a matter of time before fighting broke out, and in February 1899 full-scale war erupted. American forces were initially outnumbered, and their commander quickly called for reinforcements. Once again, regular army regiments were immediately available, so once again, buffalo soldiers were dispatched to the scene.[33]

In June 1899, the Twenty-Fifth Infantry left its posts in Colorado and Arizona and travelled to San Francisco. There the men boarded army transports bound for Manila, where they arrived in late July. For the next two years, First Sergeant Chester McNorton was one of thousands of American troops active in Central Luzon performing what the regiment's commanding officer described as "patrol and scouting duties." It was actually a brutal campaign combining occasional battles or skirmishes with constant guerrilla activity. Men of the Twenty-Fifth Infantry went on patrol to find and destroy camps or supply depots of their Filipino adversaries, ambushed Filipino fighters, and were, themselves, frequently ambushed by the Filipinos. In addition to the constant stress and danger imposed by this kind of combat, Black soldiers in the Philippines also had to deal with the psychological toll of waging a war against non-White people fighting for their independence. In the United States a significant number of African American leaders and newspapers criticized American actions in the Philippines. The *Washington Bee* called the war "a hair-brained attempt to go into the colonizing business," and Bishop Henry M. Turner of the African Methodist Episcopal Church called it "an unholy war of conquest." For their part, Filipinos used posters and leaflets to remind African Americans of the discrimination and violence they often suffered at the hands of their White countrymen and urged them to desert and join the Filipino cause. McNorton himself left no record of his feelings about the war, but another soldier in the Twenty-Fifth Infantry wrote to the *Colored American:* "I will say that we of the 25th Infantry feel rather discouraged over the fact that the sacrifice of life and health has to be made for a cause so unpopular among our people. Yet the fact that we are American soldiers instills within us the feeling and resolve to perform our duty, no matter what the consequences may be as to public sentiment."[34]

In the fall of 1901, after more than two years in the Philippines, First Sgt. McNorton returned to the United States. Most of the Twenty-Fifth Infantry remained behind, so it is unclear why McNorton returned. He may have been sent home for medical reasons; pension records indicate that he was wounded in the neck during his years in the army, but do not say when. He may have gone home, though, because his term of service was ending; he was actually mustered out aboard USAT *Kilpatrick* in route to San Francisco. Whatever the reason for his return, it did not mark the end of Chester's military career. After landing in San Francisco, he crossed the United States, perhaps to visit family, and then headed for Washington, DC, where he reenlisted in March 1902. This time he was assigned to the Twenty-Fourth Infantry and after a month of leave, during which he travelled to Christiansburg, he was dispatched to Vancouver Barracks in Washington. From there he was sent to join Company L of the Twenty-Fourth Infantry at Fort Missoula, Montana. This was the final stop in Chester McNorton's years as a buffalo soldier. On July 5, 1903, he was mustered out at Fort Missoula with a rating of "excellent" and set off for life as a civilian.[35]

He began that new life by heading east again and staying with or near his brother Stanley in Glen Jean, West Virginia. While on leave in 1902, Chester had purchased sixteen acres of land near Christiansburg and considered settling down there, but tension between Chester and his parents may have convinced him not to. Chester's father, Orville McNorton, had been facing financial problems, and in 1895 he sold his home place to Chester in order to put it beyond the reach of his creditors. Chester was supposed to sell it back once Orville settled his debts, but by 1904 Chester and Stanley had decided that their parents' interest would be better served by selling part of the property and putting the money aside to meet their needs. "We have to look out for you all in your old days," Chester wrote his parents in April 1904. "I will take the money and put it in the bank," he explained, "and as long as I am doing well and Stanley you all will not suffer for anything during your old ages." Orville clearly disliked the idea, and in 1906 he sued Chester to regain the acreage that had not already been sold.[36]

This was not the only source of tension in Chester McNorton's new life, though. His decision to marry his cousin, Lillie McNorton, seems to have upset a number of people, including his brother Stanley. Lillie was the daughter of Robert McNorton, Chester and Stanley's uncle, and had probably known them both since childhood. Lillie was eight years younger than Chester and just eleven years old when he first joined the army, so it seems unlikely they had any serious relationship that early. When Chester left the army, though, Lillie was twenty-three, and within ten months of Chester's discharge the two were romantically involved. Details of their relationship remain a mystery, but it apparently set tongues wagging in Christiansburg. Writing from Glen Jean in April 1904, Chester told his parents: "that part about Lillie McNorton and I leaving there [Christiansburg] let that be and keep it to yourselves. She is in Richmond and all of that talk is not the truth." Chester was especially anxious to keep the news from Stanley. In a postscript to his mother, Chester wrote: "Do not write to Stanley nor to Ethel [Stanley's wife] anything about it for if you do it will be that much trouble more about me and cause me to hurt you all." Two months later, despite the turmoil, Chester and Lillie were married. Both were then living in Glen Jean, and their marriage license was issued in Fayette County, but they were married in Columbus, Ohio, perhaps in an effort to hide the marriage from people in Glen Jean and Christiansburg.[37]

Trouble with his parents and his brother may have been what led Chester to head west again, or he may simply have decided after two years back east that Montana was a better place for a Black man to raise a family. Whatever their motive, in October 1905 Chester, Lillie, and their infant daughter, Tessie, arrived in Thompson Falls. At the time William McNorton was doing well there, and the local paper reported that Chester hoped to find "a piece of land to his liking" and settle there as well. Evidently, he found no land to his liking, and by 1906 the family had moved to Missoula, where Chester had spent several years during his time in the army. Chester began working there as a laborer but steadily improved his economic standing. In 1910 he bought a house lot in town and by 1917 was operating his own business as a carpet cleaner, upholsterer, and dry cleaner. He was also active in Missoula's African American community, serving as secretary of the Negro Citizens' Alliance of Missoula in 1913 and performing in "a jubilee concert" organized by the local congregation of the African Methodist Episcopal Church. His personal life was equally successful. He and Lillie had at least four more children between 1906 and 1918 and remained together until Lillie died in 1934. Chester remarried two years later, but that marriage ended in divorce by 1940. Late in his life, Chester moved to Spokane, Washington, to be closer to his children and died there in 1950.[38]

William and Chester McNorton both made new lives for themselves in Montana. Three of their brothers—Walter, Burman, and Hugh—also spent time in Montana but with much less success. Walter McNorton, born in 1873, went west during the 1890s and may have gone for health reasons. He was hospitalized in Phoenix, Arizona, in 1899 and by October 1900 was in Thompson Falls, Montana, suffering from tuberculosis. Shortly after his arrival, the Missoula newspaper reported that "by the taking of an over-dose of medicine recently his mind has at times been considerably deranged." As a result, he was first held in the county jail and then transferred to the county poor farm, where he died in November.[39]

Burman McNorton, born in 1883, was the fourth in his family to reach Montana. He went west between 1900 and 1902 and settled outside Thompson Falls. In June 1902, Burman applied for land under the Homestead Act and five years later filed notice of his intent to prove his claim. By the time his claim was proven, though, Burman had given up on ranching, moved to Ohio, and joined the army. Enlisting in January 1908, he spent just over four years in the army, all of it apparently with the Ninth Cavalry at Fort Russell, Wyoming. After leaving the army, Burman returned to Ohio and settled in Toledo, where he found work at a variety of low-skill occupations. He also found a bride, marrying Leona Day in December 1913 and beginning to raise a family with her. Between 1914 and 1920, the couple moved out of Toledo to a farm in Lucas County, west of town, and had three children. In the years that followed, Burman remained a farmer, but his family life was less stable. He and Leona divorced early in the 1920s, and his second marriage was equally short lived; he married Helen Moench in 1922 but by 1930 was divorced for the second time. After that, he remained single until his death in 1947.[40]

Hugh McNorton was the last of the brothers to go west. Born in 1889, Hugh arrived in Montana in July 1909, shortly after William returned to Thompson Falls with his new bride, India. William hired Hugh to work on the ranch but soon had "a little difficulty" with his brother and felt obliged to "chastise him." Hugh responded by robbing William at gunpoint and making his escape aboard a westbound freight train. He was quickly captured, though, and held for trial. He eventually pled guilty and served just under two years in the state penitentiary at Deer Lodge. After his release, Hugh left Montana and spent the rest of his life in Ohio and West Virginia. He never married but did have a daughter, Edith, with a woman named Lula Roberts. By 1940 he had been committed to West Virginia's "Lakin

State Hospital for the Colored Insane," and that summer he drowned trying to escape across the Ohio River.[41]

By the second quarter of the twentieth century, descendants of the families that had been enslaved at Smithfield had come far. Physically, they had spread across the United States. More importantly, they had finally been allowed to tap their full potential as human beings. The children and grandchildren of those the Prestons held in bondage had become farmers and craftsmen, warriors and poets, teachers and doctors, entrepreneurs and inventors. And it was just the beginning.

Conclusion

On December 9, 1949 the *Beckley Post-Herald* printed a funeral announcement detailing the services to be held for Mrs. Ethel Peters. Mrs. Peters, a widow, was a longtime resident of Beckley who had turned 85 just three weeks before her death. She left a son living in New York, a daughter in West Virginia, and a brother in Tennessee to mourn her passing. Left unsaid in the announcement and unknown, probably, even to Mrs. Peters, was the fact that Ethel Peters' death marked the end of an era. She was the last-known survivor of more than two-hundred Africans and African Americans enslaved at Smithfield between 1774 and 1865.

There *may* have been others still living in 1949. Many slaves can be identified only by their first names, which makes it difficult to reconstruct their histories. Even among those who can be fully identified, faulty memories and gaps in the historical record make it impossible to be certain that Ethel Peters was the last survivor among those who had been enslaved at Smithfield. Her death, however, marked the passing of the last known person whose enslavement at Smithfield, Solitude, or White Thorn can be reliably documented. Born Ethel McNorton, she was the first child of Orville and Easter Jane Fraction McNorton, and the record of her baptism at Blacksburg's Methodist church recorded the date of her birth as November 20, 1864.[1] She was just an infant when the end of the Civil War liberated her, her parents, and dozens of others enslaved at Smithfield, Solitude, and White Thorn. She certainly had no memory of the five months between her birth and her emancipation, but she had been enslaved, and her death represents a symbolic milestone in the story of slavery and the enslaved at Smithfield.

But her death certainly did not bring that story to an end. By the time Ethel Peters died, new generations descended from the families enslaved at Smithfield were already making their own way in the world. Her own children and several of her grandchildren were already adults building lives for themselves by 1949, and more would follow. That process has continued down to the present and will continue into the future. Hundreds of people across the United States today trace their descent from one or more of the people named on the 1843 inventory of James Patton Preston's estate. And their number continues to grow as each generation begets a new generation and as known descendants search out long-lost relatives and document additional branches of their family trees. The range of descendants' experiences has continued to expand too. Recent generations have certainly included farmers, miners, mechanics, and laborers, but they have also included teachers, school principals, college professors and administrators, ministers, a priest, lawyers, nurses, doctors, government workers, entrepreneurs, community activists, an award-winning saxophonist, West

Descendants of John and Easther Fraction at a 2019 reunion in Maryland. (Author's collection; photograph by Elizabeth Knapp)

Virginia's Minority Business Person of the Year, and the first Black woman to train as an American military pilot.

More than two centuries have passed since that summer day in 1759 when the *True Blue* arrived at Nanjemoy with its cargo of human misery and William Preston purchased sixteen frightened and disoriented African captives. Symbolically, if not biologically, those sixteen were the founders of a community that survived more than a century in the bonds of slavery. And as inhuman as slavery was, it could not erase the humanity of its victims. Plantation slavery has often been described as "social death" and as an institution that seriously undermined African Americans' ability to form lasting family connections. But the enslaved community at Smithfield endured; its members supported one another for nearly a century in bondage. They established families that endured, that knew their histories and through their names perpetuated the memory of members taken from them by sale or death. They possessed extraordinary strength that allowed them to survive more than a century of physical, mental, and emotional abuse. And when freedom finally came, they marshalled that same strength and began building new lives. They started with nothing but their natural intelligence, their physical strength, and their determination to succeed, and they faced enormous legal, social, and cultural barriers, but they forged ahead. Some of them failed. But many more were successful—building families and lives that brought pride and value to themselves, their communities, and their nation.

APPENDIX 1. FAMILY TREES

Individuals enslaved by the Prestons are shown in italics with their dates of birth and death.

THE FRACTION FAMILY

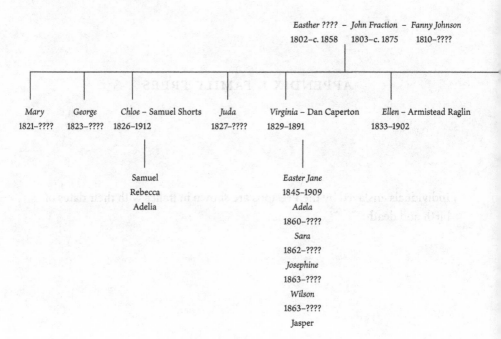

Easther ???? – John Fraction – Fanny Johnson
1802–c. 1858   1803–c. 1875   1810–????

Mary	George	Chloe – Samuel Shorts	Juda	Virginia – Dan Caperton	Ellen – Armistead Raglin
1821–????	1823–????	1826–1912	1827–????	1829–1891	1833–1902

Samuel
Rebecca
Adelia

Easter Jane
1845–1909
Adela
1860–????
Sara
1862–????
Josephine
1863–????
Wilson
1863–????
Jasper

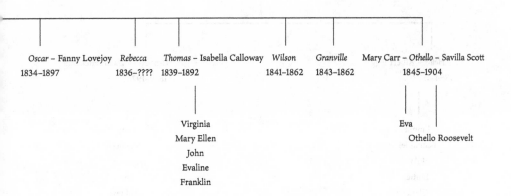

| *Oscar* – Fanny Lovejoy | *Rebecca* | *Thomas* – Isabella Calloway | *Wilson* | *Granville* | Mary Carr – *Othello* – Savilla Scott |
| 1834–1897 | 1836–???? | 1839–1892 | 1841–1862 | 1843–1862 | 1845–1904 |

Virginia
Mary Ellen
John
Evaline
Franklin

Eva
Othello Roosevelt

THE FRANKLIN FAMILY

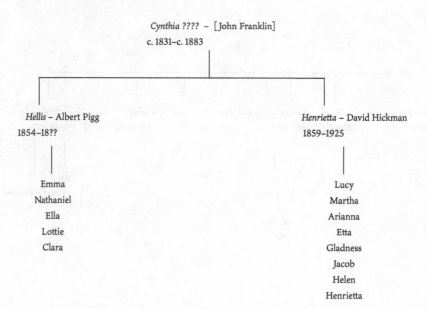

Cynthia ???? – [John Franklin]
c. 1831–c. 1883

Hellis – Albert Pigg
1854–18??

Emma
Nathaniel
Ella
Lottie
Clara

Henrietta – David Hickman
1859–1925

Lucy
Martha
Arianna
Etta
Gladness
Jacob
Helen
Henrietta

THE MOON FAMILY

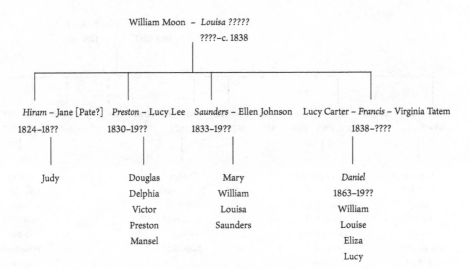

William Moon – *Louisa ?????*
????–c. 1838

Hiram – Jane [Pate?]	*Preston* – Lucy Lee	*Saunders* – Ellen Johnson	Lucy Carter – *Francis* – Virginia Tatem
1824–18??	1830–19??	1833–19??	1838–????
Judy	Douglas	Mary	*Daniel*
	Delphia	William	1863–19??
	Victor	Louisa	William
	Preston	Saunders	Louise
	Mansel		Eliza
			Lucy

THE MCNORTON FAMILY

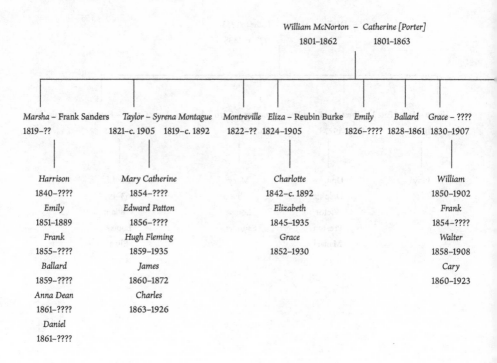

William McNorton – Catherine [Porter]
1801–1862   1801–1863

Marsha – Frank Sanders   Taylor – Syrena Montague   Montreville Eliza – Reubin Burke   Emily   Ballard   Grace – ????
1819–??   1821–c. 1905 1819–c. 1892   1822–?? 1824–1905   1826–???? 1828–1861 1830–1907

Harrison   Mary Catherine   Charlotte   William
1840–????   1854–????   1842–c. 1892   1850–1902
Emily   Edward Patton   Elizabeth   Frank
1851–1889   1856–????   1845–1935   1854–????
Frank   Hugh Fleming   Grace   Walter
1855–????   1859–1935   1852–1930   1858–1908
Ballard   James   Cary
1859–????   1860–1872   1860–1923
Anna Dean   Charles
1861–????   1863–1926
Daniel
1861–????

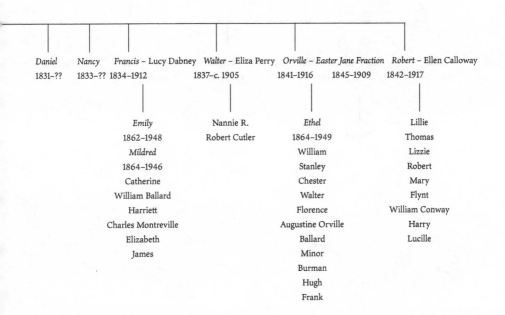

Daniel	Nancy	Francis – Lucy Dabney	Walter – Eliza Perry	Orville – Easter Jane Fraction	Robert – Ellen Calloway
1831–??	1833–??	1834–1912	1837–c. 1905	1841–1916 1845–1909	1842–1917

		Emily	Nannie R.	Ethel	Lillie
		1862–1948	Robert Cutler	1864–1949	Thomas
		Mildred		William	Lizzie
		1864–1946		Stanley	Robert
		Catherine		Chester	Mary
		William Ballard		Walter	Flynt
		Harriett		Florence	William Conway
		Charles Montreville		Augustine Orville	Harry
		Elizabeth		Ballard	Lucille
		James		Minor	
				Burman	
				Hugh	
				Frank	

THE SAUNDERS FAMILY

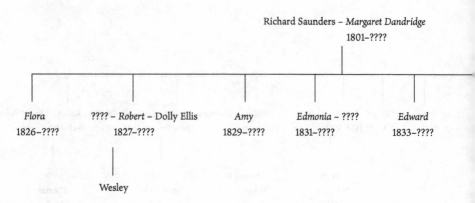

Richard Saunders – *Margaret Dandridge*
1801–????

Flora
1826–????

???? – *Robert* – Dolly Ellis
1827–????

Amy
1829–????

Edmonia – ????
1831–????

Edward
1833–????

Wesley

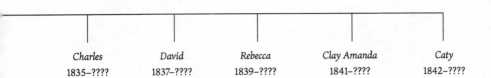

Charles
1835–????

David
1837–????

Rebecca
1839–????

Clay Amanda
1841–????

Caty
1842–????

APPENDIX 2. INDIVIDUALS ENSLAVED AT SMITHFIELD, SOLITUDE, OR WHITE THORN, 1774–1865

The list below includes 226 individuals named among those enslaved at Smithfield, Solitude, or White Thorn between 1774 and 1865. Surnames inside brackets are the married names of women whose birth names remain unknown.

NAME	SURNAME	FIRST RECORD	BORN
Abram		1782	1766–82
Adela	Capers	1862	1860
Aggy		1782	1766–82
Alex		1855	
Alfred		1806	
Allice		1866	1864
Amanda	Saunders	1843	1841
Ambrose		1782	1766–82
Amy	Saunders	1843	1841
Andy		1843	1818
Anna Dean	Sanders	1867	1861
Anny/Amy		1806	
Anthony		1826	1820
Ballard	McNorton	1843	1828
Ballard	Sanders	1867	1859
Becky		1806	1790
Betsy		1826	1818

NAME	SURNAME	FIRST RECORD	BORN
Bett		1782	1766–82
Beverly		1843	1837
Biddy		1843	1840
Billy		1806	
Bob		1782	1766–82
Caroline		1843	1832
Cate	[McNorton]	1826	1801
Caty	Fisher	1826	
Caty	Saunders	1843	1842
Charity		1857	
Charles		1806	
Charles	McNorton	1866	1863
Charles	Saunders	1843	1835
Charles (Dan)		1826	1806
Charlotte	Burke	1843	1842
Chloe		1806	1786
Chloe	Fraction	1826	1826
Clary		1782	1766–82
Clay		1843	1783
Clay Amanda	Saunders	1843	1841
Cyrena		1857	
Cynthia		1782	1778
Cynthia	[Franklin]	1843	1831
Daniel	McNorton	1843	1831
Daniel	Jones	1843	1843
Daniel	Sanders	1867	1861
David	Saunders	1843	1837
Davy		1806	
Delice		1860	
Diana		1843	1821
Doll		1782	pre-1760

NAME	SURNAME	FIRST RECORD	BORN
Easter Jane	Fraction	1862	1845
Easther	[Fraction]	1826	1802
Easther, "daut of M"		1843	1833
Edmonia		1826	1820
Edmonia	Saunders	1843	1831
Edmund		1843	1810
Edward	McNorton	1866	1856
Edward	Saunders	1843	1833
Eliza	McNorton	1826	1824
Eliza		1843	1828
Elizabeth	Burke	1859	1845
Ellen		1826	
Ellen	Fraction	1843	1833
Emily	McNorton	1843	1826
Emily	Sanders	1867	1851
Esaw		1843	1828
Esther		1783	1783
Ethel	McNorton	1866	1864
Fanny		1782	1766–82
Fanny	Johnson	1852	1809
Festus		1858	1857
Flora		1782	1760–66
Flora	Saunders	1826	1826
Francis		1826	1824
Francis	Moon	1843	1838
Frank/John	McNorton	1843	1834
Frank	Sanders	1867	1855
Gena		1855	
George	Fraction	1826	1823
George		1782	1766–82
Grace	Burke	1857	1852

NAME	SURNAME	FIRST RECORD	BORN
Grace	McNorton	1843	1830
Granville		1806	
Granville	Fraction	1862	1843
Green		1853	
Hannah		1782	1766–82
Harmon		1852	
Harriet		1826	
Harrison	Sanders	1843	1840
Harry		1782	pre-1760
Hellis	Franklin	1862	1854
Henrietta	Franklin	1862	1859
Henry	Johnson	1853	1830
Henry	Boldin	1857	
Hiram	Moon	1826	1824
Hugh	McNorton	1859	1859
Isaac		1816	1811
Isaac		1843	1825
Isaac, "son N"		1843	1837
Izy		1855	
Jack		1782	pre-1760
Jack		1806	1783
Jacob		1843	1828
James		1826	
James		1843	1828
James	McNorton	1866	1860
Janey		1826	
Jem		1782	pre-1760
Jem		1782	1766–82
Jenny		1782	pre-1760
Joe		1782	1766–82
Joe		1857	

NAME	SURNAME	FIRST RECORD	BORN
John		1806	
John	Fraction	1826	1803
John	Smith	1863	
Jones		1855	
Joseph		1843	1841
Josephine	Capers	1867	1863
Joshua		1843	1826
Juda	Fraction	1843	1827
Judy		1783	1783
Judy		1816	1807
Juny		1856	
Katy		1852	
Lewis		1806	1790
Lewis		1854	
Lively		1843	1821
Lizzy		1854	
Louisa	[Moon]	1826	
Lucinda		1826	1824
Lucius		1806	
Lucy		1806	
Lucy		1816	1812
Margaret		1843	1842
Maria		1826	
Maria	Lewis	1866	1841
Mariah		1843	1834
Marsha	McNorton	1826	1819
Martha		1823	1816
Martha		1843	1837
Mary	Carr	1861	1839
Mary	Fraction	1826	1821
Mary	McNorton	1866	1854

NAME	SURNAME	FIRST RECORD	BORN
Mary Ann		1843	1806
Maud		1857	
May		1859	
Mike	Menser	1826	1787
Montgomery		1853	
Montreville	McNorton	1826	1822
Moses		1782	pre-1760
Moses		1826	1816
Nancy		1806	
Nancy		1826	1817
Nancy		1856	
Nancy	McNorton	1843	1833
Nancy Jane		1843	1842
Nanny		1782	1760–66
Nanny		1816	1810
Ned		1782	pre-1760
Ned		1782	pre-1760
Nelly		1782	1773
Nelson		1782	1766–82
Oceola		1843	1838
Orange		1843	1842
Orville	McNorton	1843	1841
Oscar		1806	
Oscar	Fraction	1843	1834
Othello		1806	1797
Othello	Fraction	1856	1845
Patrick		1854	
Peggy	Dandridge	1806	1801
Peter		1774	
Peter		1782	1781
Peter		1826	1823

NAME	SURNAME	FIRST RECORD	BORN
Peyton		1843	1831
Philip		1826	1787
Pleasant		1852	
Preston	Moon	1843	1830
Primus, "Old"		1782	pre-1760
Primus, "Yg"		1782	1766–82
Rachel		1782	pre-1760
Rebecca		1826	
Rebecca	Fraction	1843	1836
Rebecca	Saunders	1843	1839
Reuben		1782	1773
Reuben		1816	1811
Reuben		1855	
Rhena		1843	1828
Robert	McNorton	1843	1842
Robert	Saunders	1843	1827
Rose		1843	1839
Rosey		1806	
Ruben	Smith	1866	1863
Sally		1806	
Sally		1843	1835
Sam		1782	pre-1760
Sam		1806	1789
Sarah		1782	pre-1760
Sarah	Capers	1867	1862
Sarah Jane		1843	1839
Saunders	Moon	1843	1833
Silvia		1782	pre-1760
Silvy		1816	1814
Spencer		1854	
Stephen		1806	1785

NAME	SURNAME	FIRST RECORD	BORN
Sukey		1806	1792
Susan		1843	1841
Sydney		1852	
Syrena	Montague	1826	1819
Taylor	McNorton	1826	1821
Thomas		1816	1812
Tom		1782	1766–82
Tom	Banks	1853	1826
Tom	Fraction	1843	1839
Tom	King	1852	
Ugenia		1843	1841
Ursula		1826	
Virginia	Fraction	1843	1829
Walter	McNorton	1843	1837
Wesley		1826	
Will		1782	1766–82
William	Dandridge	1823	
William	McNorton	1826	1801
William	Poindexter	1866	1838
Willie		1853	
Willis		1826	1814
Wilson	Capers	1867	1863
Wilson	Fraction	1843	1841

❖ NOTES ❖

ABBREVIATIONS

1865 Census   "Census Return of the Colored Population of Montgomery Co., State of Va. August 1865," reel 198, Records of the Field Offices for the State of Virginia, Bureau of Refugees, Freedmen, and Abandoned Lands, 1865–72, Microfilm Publication 1913, Record Group 105, National Archives, Washington, DC.

1867 Census   "Census Returns of Colored Population of Montgomery County, State of Virginia [1867]," reel 68, Records of the Field Offices for the State of Virginia, Bureau of Refugees, Freedmen, and Abandoned Lands, 1865–72, Microfilm Publication 1913, Record Group 105, National Archives, Washington, DC.

BRFAL-FOVA   Records of the Field Offices for the State of Virginia, Bureau of Refugees, Freedmen, and Abandoned Lands, 1865–72, Microfilm Publication 1913, Record Group 105, National Archives, Washington, DC.

FCCH   Fayette County Courthouse, Fayetteville, West Virginia.

Fullerton   "Nigger Bill" (William McNorton), Box 5, Folder 5, Neil Fullerton Research Collection, Montana Historical Society, Helena, Montana.

LOV   Library of Virginia, Richmond, Virginia.

MCCH   Montgomery County Courthouse, Christiansburg, Virginia.

MC Cohabitation   "Register of Colored Persons of Montgomery County, State of Virginia, Cohabiting Together as Husband and Wife on 27th February, 1866," Montgomery County Clerk of the Circuit Court's Office, Christiansburg, Virginia.

MSA   Maryland State Archives, Annapolis, Maryland

PCW Pensions   Federal Military Pension Application—Pre–Civil War, Record Group 15, Department of Veterans Affairs, National Archives, Washington, DC.

Preston Memoranda   Francis Preston Memoranda Book, Folder 3, Preston Family Papers, Gray Collection, Mss. A. P937k, Filson Historical Society, Lexington, Kentucky.

RCCH   Roanoke County Courthouse, Salem, Virginia.

SCCV   Southern Claims Commission Approved Claims, 1871–1880: Virginia, Microfilm Publication 2094, Record Group 217, National Archives, Washington, DC.

USCT Pensions   Civil War and Later Pension Files, Department of Veterans Affairs, Record Group 15, National Archives, Washington, DC.

VHS   Virginia Historical Society, Richmond, Virginia.

VT   Special Collections, Newman Library, Virginia Tech, Blacksburg, Virginia.

INTRODUCTION

1. For a summary of voyages made by the *True Blue,* see Trans-Atlantic Slave Trade Database.
2. Thorp, *Facing Freedom,* 10–12.

1. SLAVERY COMES TO SMITHFIELD

1. Information about the *True Blue* comes from the Trans-Atlantic Slave Trade Database. For a discussion of the Atlantic slave trade in this era, see Thomas, *The Slave Trade;* Klein, *The Atlantic Slave Trade;* Rediker, *The Slave Ship.*
2. Thomas, *The Slave Trade,* 291–408; Klein, *The Atlantic Slave Trade,* 103–29; *Maryland Gazette,* August 16, 1759, http://aomol.msa.maryland.gov/html/mdgazette.html.

3. Thomas, *The Slave Trade*, 409–30; Klein, *The Atlantic Slave Trade*, 130–60.

4. Klein, *The Atlantic Slave Trade*, 140; details of the *True Blue*'s voyage and cargo in 1759 available from the Trans-Atlantic Slave Trade Database.

5. Osborn, "William Preston: Origins of a Backcountry Political Career"; Mitchell, *Commercialism and Frontier*, 25–36, 52–55, 59–65; Nelson, *Pharsalia*, 30–39.

6. Craven, *White, Red, and Black*, 1–37; Morgan, *American Slavery, American Freedom*, 92–130; Rutman and Rutman, *A Place in Time*, 36–47; Billings, "The Law of Servants and Slaves in Seventeenth-Century Virginia."

7. Osborn, "William Preston: Origins of a Backcountry Political Career," 15–23; Glanville, "William Preston the Surveyor."

8. Nelson, *Pharsalia*, 33; Glanville, "William Preston the Surveyor," 58–60; Osborn, "William Preston, 1727–1783: The Making of a Frontier Elite," 124.

9. Receipt for slaves, August 28, 1759, folder 301, Preston Family of Virginia Papers, Library of Congress, Manuscript Division; Osborn, "William Preston, 1727–1783: The Making of a Frontier Elite," 124; Bergstrom, "Nothing So Certain."

10. Receipt for slaves, August 28, 1759, folder 301, Preston Family of Virginia Papers, Library of Congress, Manuscript Division; Mitchell, *Commercialism and Frontier*, 128; "An Act Concerning Tithables," Hening, *The Statutes at Large*, 6:40–44; Osborn, "William Preston, 1727–1783: The Making of a Frontier Elite," 124–25.

11. Osborn, "William Preston, 1727–1783: The Making of a Frontier Elite," 125–27 and 164–73; McCleskey, *The Road to Black Ned's Forge*, 128.

12. Mitchell, *Commercialism and Frontier*, 13–25; Lindon, *Virginia's Montgomery County*, 19–41.

13. Glanville, "William Preston the Surveyor," 58–63.

14. Isaac, *The Transformation of Virginia*, 34–42; Nelson, *Pharsalia*, 51–62; Osborn, William Preston, 1727–1783: The Making of a Frontier Elite," 199–201; Willis, "Genesis and Dissolution."

15. Osborn, "William Preston, 1727–1783: The Making of a Frontier Elite," 297–300 and 355–60.

16. Ibid., 355–60 and 375; Willis, "Genesis and Dissolution," 31; Herndon, "Hemp in Colonial Virginia."

17. Osborn, "William Preston, 1727–1783: The Making of a Frontier Elite," 358.

18. Ibid., 125, 375; "List of William Preston's taxable property to be returned to Capt. James Byran by the 10th April 1782" and "A List of William Prestons Property [May 1783]," both in Montgomery County, Miscellaneous Court Records, 1750–1861, BC 1048924, LOV.

19. "List of William Preston's taxable property to be returned to Capt. James Byran by the 10th April 1782" and "A List of William Prestons Property [May 1783]," both in Montgomery County, Miscellaneous Court Records, 1750–1861, BC 1048924, LOV.

20. Ibid.; List of slaves distributed in October 1816, Preston Memoranda.

21. For a fuller discussion of the process by which enslaved Africans preserved and modified their traditional cultures in Virginia, see Walsh, *From Calabar to Carter's Grove*, 81–170.

22. Osborn, "William Preston, 1727–1783: The Making of a Frontier Elite," 381–82; Will Book B: 55, MCCH; Deed Book P: 186, MCCH.

23. Will Book B: 55, MCCH. Growth in the enslaved population at Smithfield calculated by comparing the 1783 tax list (Montgomery County, Miscellaneous Court Records, 1750–1861, BC 1048924, LOV) to the slaves named by Francis Preston in 1806 ("A list of the negroes given up by my mother when the Tripartite or Compromise agreement was entered into by the Heirs Present," Preston Memoranda). Growth is also evident in personal property tax rolls, though the tax rolls counted only those above age twelve; see Montgomery County Personal Property Tax Records, LOV.

24. Preston Memoranda. In a report prepared for Historic Smithfield, Phillip Troutman concluded there were three divisions between 1783 and 1816: one sometime between 1790 and 1806, a second in 1806, and a third in 1816; Phillip D. Troutman, "Research Report One: Filson Historical Society Material on Smithfield & Slavery," December 2000, Smithfield Library, Historic Smithfield, Blacksburg, VA. A close reading of the lists, however, suggests there were just two divisions: 1806 and 1816. Montgomery County's personal property tax lists also suggest there were just two. William Preston's estate continued to pay taxes on twenty or more slaves over the age of twelve until 1801. In 1802, the year Peggy Preston married, that number did drop to thirteen, but it remained there until 1806. The estate then ceased to appear in tax records at all, suggesting the estate was divided that year; see Montgomery County Personal Property Tax Records, LOV.

25. U.S. Census 1810; Preston Memoranda. Slaves retained by Susanna Preston are identified in "An Inventory of the personal estate of Wm. Preston deceased as left by Susanna Preston his widow & relect & not inventoried heretofore," MC Wills, 1827, MCCH.

26. Preston Memoranda; "An Inventory of the personal estate of Wm. Preston deceased as left by Susanna Preston his widow & relect & not inventoried heretofore," MC Wills, 1827, MCCH; U.S. Census 1820.

27. Preston Memoranda; "An Inventory of the personal estate of Wm. Preston deceased as left by Susanna Preston his widow & relect & not inventoried heretofore," MC Wills, 1827, MCCH; U.S. Censuses 1870, 1880, 1900, 1910.

28. Will Book 4: 269, MCCH. This bond, executed by James Patton Preston in October 1826, identifies by name thirty-nine enslaved individuals pledged to satisfy the $8,047 guaranteed by the bond, but the list omits several individuals who are known to have passed to Preston during the various divisions of his father's estate and to have still been alive in 1826.

2. THE ENSLAVED PEOPLE OF SMITHFIELD

1. "J.P. Preston Appraisement," Will Book 7: 130, MCCH.

2. Willis, "Genesis and Dissolution"; Wedin, "A Summary of 19th-Century Smithfield, Part 1." The distribution of slaves after 1843 is based on the Accounts for William B. Preston, Robert T. Preston, and James F. Preston, Harvey Black Medical Accounts, Box 7, Black-Kent-Apperson Papers, Ms1974-003, VT; Accounts of William Ballard Preston with Harvey Black, James Otey, and Henry Ribble, Adms. of William Ballard Preston v. Heirs of William Ballard Preston, Chancery 1900-014 (originally nos. 2822 and 3495), MCCH; "Montgomery County Deaths, 1853–1868," MCCH; Estate inventory of James F. Preston, Will Book 9: 421, MCCH; 1865 Census; MC Cohabitation. Personal property tax records suggest that Catharine inherited seven of her father's slaves, though only six can be identified by name; see Tax lists for 1848 and 1849, Montgomery County Personal Property Tax Records, LOV.

3. "A List of William Prestons Property," May 1783, Montgomery County, Miscellaneous Court Records, 1750–1861, BC 1048924, LOV; U.S. census 1860, slave schedule.

4. Preston to James McDowell, December 5, 1801, Smithfield Preston Foundation Papers, Ms1997-002, VT; Wm. Wade v. Adm. of Wm. Ballard Preston, Chancery 1863-001 (originally no. 189), MCCH; "Wm. Ballard Preston Settlement," Will Book 10: 279, MCCH.

5. Wedin, "A Summary of 19th-Century Smithfield, Part 1," 83–89.

6. Woodward, Mary Chestnut's Civil War, 29.

7. Fullerton Collection. William McNorton's date of birth varies from record to record but seems to have been August of 1866 or 1867.

8. Genovese, Roll, Jordan, Roll, 463–64; Gutman, The Black Family, 75–80; Walsh, From Calabar to Carter's Grove, 83–85.

9. Gutman, *The Black Family,* especially pages 3–326; Escott, *Slavery Remembered;* Manfra and Dykstra, "Serial Marriage and the Origins of the Black Stepfamily"; Burton, *In My Father's House Are Many Mansions,* 148–202; Stevenson, *Life in Black and White,* 159–319; Dunaway, *The African American Family,* 51–178; Pargas, *The Quarters and the Fields.*

10. Deposition of Brandon Leftwich in Fuqua v. Fuqua, Chancery 1876-006 (originally no. 512), MCCH.

11. For a fuller discussion of naming patterns among enslaved Africans and African Americans, see Gutman, *The Black Family,* 185–201 and Walsh, *From Calabar to Carter's Grove,* 159–70.

12. Gutman, *The Black Family,* especially pages 3–326; Stevenson, *Life in Black and White,* 159–319; Dunaway, *The African American Family;* Pargas, *The Quarters and the Fields.*

13. Thorp, "Cohabitation Registers."

14. John Fraction was identified by name in 1826 as part of "the personal estate of Wm. Preston deceased as left by Susannah Preston, his widow." An earlier list of slaves "ret[ained] by Mrs. Preston" when William Preston's estate was initially divided includes only one named John, who was identified as "Jacks John," to distinguish him from another John who went to William Preston's daughter, Susanna, and her husband, Nathaniel Hart. Unfortunately, William Preston's estate included two men named Jack. One was at least twenty-one years old in 1783 and seems to have died by 1806, while the other was born in October 1783 and was still alive in 1816. It is impossible to be sure which of the two was the father of "Jacks John," but John Fraction was, apparently, either a second- or third-generation Smithfield slave; see Will Book 4: 339, MCCH; Preston Memoranda.

15. "List of William Preston's taxable property to be returned to Capt. James Byran by the 10th April 1782" and "A List of William Prestons Property [May 1783]," both in Montgomery County, Miscellaneous Court Records, 1750–1861, BC 1048924, LOV; Preston Memoranda.

16. Ibid. An oral history recorded in 1977 by Richard Dickenson says that Catherine McNorton's birth name was Porter; see "Interview with Mrs. Nettie Anderson," Box 11, Series 5, Richard B. Dickenson Papers, Ms. 2011-043, VT.

17. "Interview with Mrs. Nettie Anderson," Box 11, Series 5, Richard B. Dickenson Papers, Ms. 2011-043, VT; 1867 Census; Marriage license of Emily Sanders, Marriage Licenses, 1867: 68, MCCH; U.S. Censuses 1870, 1880, and 1900; Death certificate of Grace Burke Strothers, Ohio Deaths, 1908–1953, familysearch.org.

18. Will Book 4: 339, MCCH; "J.P. Preston Appraisement," Will Book 7: 130, MCCH; MC Cohabitation.

19. This identification is based on the 1876 marriage license of Frank Moon, who identified his parents as "William & Louisa Moon"; see Marriage Licenses 1876: 136, MCCH. Louisa also appears with Hiram, her eldest son, among the enslaved individuals named in an 1826 deed of trust provided by James Patton Preston to secure a bond; see Will Book 4: 269, MCCH.

20. Vaughn, "Blacks in Virginia"; Thorndale, "The Virginia Census of 1619"; Sluiter, "New Light on the '20"; Thornton, "The African Experience"; Heinegg, *Free African Americans*, 1–8; Russell, *The Free Negro in Virginia*, 9–16 and 42–87; Berlin, *Slaves Without Masters*, 139 and 140–41; Ely, *Israel on the Appomattox*, 35, 37–38. Chapter 111, section 62, in *The Revised Code of the Laws of Virginia* (1819) shows this change and says it was passed in March 1819, while Ellen Eslinger says the change came in 1815; see Eslinger, "Free Black Residency in Two Antebellum Counties," 271.

21. Berlin, *Slaves Without Masters*, 92–99; West, *Family or Freedom*, 33–34; Ely, *Israel on the Appomattox*; quoted in Von Daacke, *Freedom Has a Face*, 41.

22. U.S. Censuses 1810, 1820, and 1830; File of William Moon (sometimes "Moore"), SCCV; "Book of Free Negroes," MCCH; Deed Book L: 309, MCCH; Will Book 6: 19, MCCH.

23. Tax lists for 1839, 1840, and 1841, Montgomery County Personal Property Tax Records, LOV; Court Order Book 29: 73 and 93, MCCH; "J.P. Preston Appraisement," Will Book 7: 130, MCCH; Marriage license of Frank Moon, Marriage Licenses, 1876: 136, MCCH.

24. George Gilmer to Mary Gilmer, August 20, 1847, 1969.51.424, Breck-inridge Collection, History Museum of Western Virginia, Roanoke. The distribution of slaves among the heirs of James Patton Preston can be estab-lished from the following records: Accounts of William Ballard Preston, James F. Preston, and Robert T. Preston, Harvey Black Medical Accounts, Box 7, Black, Kent, and Apperson Family Papers, Ms1974-003, VT; Accounts of William Ballard Preston with Harvey Black, James Otey, and Henry Ribble, Adms. of William Ballard Preston v. Heirs of William Ballard Preston, Chancery 1900-014 (originally nos. 2822 and 3495), MCCH; and MC Cohabitation.

25. U.S. Census 1860, slave schedule; MC Cohabitation. Architectural and archaeological evidence from Solitude and White Thorn suggests that both Robert T. and James F. Preston expanded or built various structures on their estates during the late 1840s and throughout the 1850s; see Pulice, "The Log Outbuilding at Solitude," 7–10; White Thorn registration form

for the National Register of Historic Places, June 1988, https://www.dhr
.virginia.gov/historic-registers/150-5021/.

26. MC Cohabitation. At least one other couple seems to have married
and lived together at White Thorn between 1847 and 1865. Virginia Fraction married a man named Dan Caperton, who probably belonged to Sarah
Anne Caperton Preston, the wife of James F. Preston, and died before the
cohabitation register was compiled; see Marriage license of Wilson Capers,
Marriage Licenses, 1882: 98, MCCH.

27. MC Cohabitation.

28. Mary Carr Fraction and William Poindexter each named William Ballard Preston as their former owner but reported that they had been born
in Henry County, where Preston owned three plantations and at least 150
slaves. Preston may have acquired them when he married Lucinda Redd
and brought them to Smithfield, but it is also possible that they lived apart
from their spouses until emancipation and then joined them in Montgomery County; see MC Cohabitation.

29. "J.P. Preston Appraisement," Will Book 7: 130, MCCH; MC Cohabitation. On the inventory, one can use the ages of adults and those of their
oldest known children to estimate the ages at which the parents married,
but the oldest known child of a couple may not actually have been its first
born. As for the cohabitation register, informants were asked their age and
the "date cohabitation began," but ages may still be unreliable because the
register does not distinguish between first marriages and later marriages.

3. LIFE AND WORK IN THE QUARTERS

1. Worsham, *Smithfield*, 57–58; Will Book 10: 116, MCCH.

2. Personal communication Kerri Moseley-Hobbs; Bongmba, *The Wiley-
Blackwell Companion to African Religions*, 144–47; Azaare, "Sacred Trees in
Ghana."

3. Photos of White Thorn provided by Glencoe Museum, Radford, VA;
Pulice, "The Log Outbuilding at Solitude," 55–64.

4. Application of Greenfield for inclusion on the National Register of Historic Places, 011-0026, prepared by Michael J. Pulice and John R. Kern,
Virginia Department of Historic Resources, April 2010, https://www.dhr
.virginia.gov/VLR_to_transfer/PDFNoms/011-0026_Greenfield_2010
_NRHP_FINAL.pdf.

5. Genovese, *Roll, Jordan, Roll*, 535–40; Pargas, "Various Means of Providing
for Their Own Tables."

6. Pulice, "The Log Outbuilding at Solitude," 63; James Barnett v. Chapman C. Johnson et al, Common Law A-5276, MCCH.

7. Adms. of William Ballard Preston v. Heirs of William Ballard Preston, Chancery 1900-014 (originally nos. 2822 and 3495), MCCH; Accounts of William Ballard Preston, James F. Preston, and Robert T. Preston, Harvey Black Medical Account Book, Box 7, Black, Kent, and Apperson Family Papers, Ms1974-003, VT.

8. Ibid.; Tunc, "The Mistress, the Midwife, and the Medical Doctor."

9. "List of Official Members and Records of Quarterly Meetings, June 2, 1827 to Dec. 23, 1854," and "Register of Christiansburg Station, Roanoke District, Baltimore Conf., M.E. Church, South, [1861–85]," both in St. Paul United Methodist Church, Christiansburg, VA; "Record of Baptisms, 1859–1878," Box 5, Folder 1, Whisner Memorial Methodist Church Records, Ms 64-003, VT; "Records of the Church Session, 1827," Christiansburg Presbyterian Church, Christiansburg, VA; "Records of the Session of the Blacksburg Church," Blacksburg Presbyterian Church, Blacksburg, VA; "Inventory of Membership by Race of Baptist Churches in Virginia in 1860 by County and City," in Whitt, "Free Indeed!" 2928–37.

10. Loveland, *Southern Evangelicals and the Social Order*, 219–56; Touchstone, "Planters and Slave Religion in the Deep South," 99–126; Richey, Rowe, and Schmidt, *The Methodist Experience in America*, 158–60; Whitt, "Free Indeed!" 2783–937.

11. "Record of Baptisms, 1859–1878," Box 5, Whisner Memorial Methodist Church Records, Ms 64-003, VT; Donald, "Blacksburg Methodist Churches"; Owen, "By Design."

12. "List of Official Members and Records of Quarterly Meetings, June 2, 1827, to December 23, 1854," and "Register of Christiansburg Station, Roanoke District, Baltimore Conf., M.E. Church, South," St. Paul United Methodist Church, Christiansburg, VA; "Recording Stewards Book, 1859–1880," Box 3, Folder 6, Whisner Memorial Methodist Church Records, Ms 64-003, VT.

13. Ibid.

14. "Record of Baptisms, 1859–1878," Box 5, Whisner Memorial Methodist Church Records, Ms 64-003, VT; Mathews, *Slavery and Methodism*, 66; Miller, "Slaves and Southern Catholicism," 127–52 (especially 135); Loveland, *Southern Evangelicals and the Social Order*, 210–11.

15. Raboteau, *Canaan Land*, 42–60; quoted in Perdue, Barden, and Phillips, *Weevils in the Wheat*, 94 and 124.

16. *(Montgomery) Messenger*, February 7, 1879; "Record of Baptisms, 1859–1878," Box 5, Whisner Memorial Methodist Church Records, Ms 64-003,

VT; MC Cohabitation; Leftwich et al v. Pattersons' Admr., Chancery, 1899-048 (originally no. 1772), MCCH.

17. Lindon, *Virginia's Montgomery County*, 163–69; Noe, *Southwest Virginia's Railroad*, 11–30.

18. Herndon, "Hemp in Colonial Virginia," 93.

19. U.S. Censuses 1850 and 1860, schedule of agriculture; Worsham, *Smithfield*, 32 and 59.

20. MC Cohabitation; U.S. Census 1860, slave schedule.

21. MC Cohabitation; Pargas, *The Quarters and the Fields*, 39–62.

22. Population schedules of the U.S. census identify overseers in 1850 and 1860; Mary Elizabeth Caperton to George Henry Caperton, May 9, 1861, Caperton Family Papers, 1729–1973, Section 8, George Henry Caperton, Mss1 C1716 a 176–354, VHS; Janie Milton transcript, Box 1, Folder 38, John Nicolay Papers, Ms87-027, VT; William Ballard Preston to William H. Linkous, May 4, 1861, Preston Family Papers, 1773–1862. Section 14, Correspondence, 1840–1862, of William Ballard Preston (1805–1862), Mss1 P9267 d 296–708, VHS; Adms. of William Ballard Preston v. William Linkous, Chancery, 1869-006 (originally no. 263), MCCH.

23. Janie Milton transcript, Box 1, Folder 38, John Nicolay Papers, Ms 87-027, VT.

24. U.S. Censuses 1870 and 1880; Wedin, "The Preston Cemetery"; Mary Eliza Caperton to George Henry Caperton, May 27, 1861, Caperton Family Papers, 1729–1973, Section 8, George Henry Caperton Mss1 C1716 a 176–354, VHS; James F. Preston to Charles Gardner, August 21, 1861, quoted in Wedin, "A Summary of 19th-Century Smithfield, Part 2," 83.

25. "Wm. Ballard Preston Settlement," Will Book 10: 279, MCCH; John Preston to William Preston, May 1795, quoted in Troutman, "Research Report One," Smithfield Library, Historic Smithfield; Holmberg, *Dear Brother*, 125; Wallace, "The First Regiment of Virginia Volunteers"; Pension application of Taylor McNorton, PCW Pensions; Will of James F. Preston, Will Book 9: 388 MCCH.

26. For a fuller discussion of slave hiring in Virginia, see Zaborney, *Slaves for Hire*.

27. "Wm. Ballard Preston Settlement," Will Book 10: 279, MCCH; Eric Arnesen, *Brotherhoods of Color*, 6–7; Kornweibel, *Railroads in the African American Experience*, 11–24; Schermerhorn, *Money over Mastery, Family over Freedom*, 164–201; quoted in Mitchell to Buford, October 21, 1851, John Quincy Adams Buford Papers, 1844–1865, Mss 9782, Albert and Shirley Small Special Collections, University of Virginia Library; U.S. Census 1860, slave schedule, Montgomery County, VA.

28. Dew, *Bond of Iron*, 29–31; McClesky, *The Road to Black Ned's Forge*, 67–68; Whisonant, "Geology and History of the Civil War Iron Industry."

29. Ibid.; "Wm. Ballard Preston Settlement," Will Book 10: 279, MCCH.

30. Will Book B: 55, MCCH; Hammit to Preston, August 10, 1820, transcript at Smithfield Library, Historic Smithfield of an original in the Virginia Historical Society.

31. Speech by William B. Preston to the House of Delegates, January 16, 1832, available at *Encyclopedia Virginia.*

32. Troutman, "Research Report One," Smithfield Library, Historic Smithfield; April 1 and June 3, 1861, Order Book, Co. Court Com. Law & Chancy. 1859–1868, MCCH; Inventory of James F. Preston, Will Book 9: 421, MCCH.

4. WAR COMES TO SMITHFIELD

1. *New Star* (Christiansburg, VA), August 25, 1860, September 15, 1860, November 3, 1860, March 30, 1861, and April 27, 1861.

2. Mary Eliza Caperton to George Henry Caperton, May 9, 1861, Caperton Family Papers, 1729–1973, Section 8, George Henry Caperton, Mss1 C1716 a 176–354, VHS.

3. *New Star*, September 1, 1860, September 15, 1860, November 24, 1860, and April 27, 1861; Order Book, Co. Court Com. Law & Chancy, 1859–1868, May Term 1861, MCCH; Preston to Linkous, May 4, 1861, Correspondence, 1840–1862, of William Ballard Preston (1805–1862), Preston Family Papers, 1773–1862, Section 14, Mss1 P9267 d 296–708, VHS.

4. Mary Eliza Caperton to George Henry Caperton, May 14 and May 27, 1861, Caperton Family Papers, 1729–1973, Section 8, George Henry Caperton, Mss1 C1716 a 176–354, VHS; Commonwealth v. Price, Criminal, A-655, MCCH.

5. "Wm. Ballard Preston Settlement," Will Book 10: 279, MCCH; Preston to Linkous, May 4, 1861, Correspondence, 1840–1862, of William Ballard Preston (1805–1862), Preston Family Papers, 1773–1862, Section 14, Mss1 P9267 d 296–708, VHS; Adms. of William Ballard Preston v. Heirs of William Ballard Preston, Chancery, 1900-104 (originally nos. 2822 and 3495); Bruce, Tyler, and Morton, *History of Virginia*, 6: 412.

6. MC Cohabitation.

7. Ibid.; Montgomery County Deaths, 1853–1868, MCCH.

8. Johnson, *The United States Army Invades the New River Valley*; Duncan, *Lee's Endangered Left*, 43–84; Grimsley, *And Keep Moving On*, 94–102; Wilson, "The Dublin Raid," 92–120; Lizzie Black Apperson quoted in Johnson, *The United States Army Invades the New River Valley*, 59; Caroline

Meek Thomas to Jane Meek Hoge, May 26, 1864, Box 1, Folder 6, William E. Hoge Family Papers, Mss 2003-019, VT.

9. Johnson, *The United States Army Invades the New River Valley;* File of William Moon (sometimes "Moore"), SCCV; personal communication Laura Wedin.

10. Statement of Waller Staples and Accounts of Henry Ribble, both in Adms. of William Ballard Preston v. Heirs of William Ballard Preston, Chancery, 1900-014 (originally nos. 2822 and 3495), MCCH; "Wm. Ballard Preston Settlement," Will Book 10: 279, MCCH.

11. Levin, *Searching for Black Confederates,* 12–36; Will Book 9: 388, MCCH.

12. Wedin, "A Summary of 19th-Century Smithfield, Part 2," 86–87; Will Book 9: 388, MCCH; Harvey Black to Mary Black, April 28, 1862, in McMullen, *A Surgeon with Stonewall Jackson,* 28–29 and 152.

13. Nelson, "Confederate Slave Impressment Legislation"; Brewer, *The Confederate Negro,* 3–16; Martinez, *Confederate Slave Impressment in the Upper South,* 1–18; Thorp, "Soldiers, Servants, and Very Interested Bystanders"; *Acts of the General Assembly of the State of Virginia Passed at Called Session, 1862,* chap. 2; December 19, 1862, September 7, 1863, February 6, 1864, January 7, February 6, and February 7, 1865, Order Book, Co. Court Com. Law & Chancy, 1859–1868, MCCH.

14. Levin, *Searching for Black Confederates,* 68–176.

15. Levine, *Confederate Emancipation.*

16. Luke and Smith, *Soldiering for Freedom,* 14–19; Hunter, *Bound in Wedlock,* 166–67.

17. Chris J. Hartley, *Stoneman's Raid,* 115–67. Individual slaves were identified using the records of men serving in the Fortieth USCT, which was formed, in part, by former slaves sent by Stoneman from Germantown to East Tennessee; C.S. Schaeffer to W. Austin, March 23, 1867, BRFAL-FOVA, reel 67; and Moche, *Families of Grace through 1900,* I: 96.

18. Accounts of Dr. Harvey Black, Adms. of William Ballard Preston v. Heirs of William Ballard Preston, Chancery, 1900-014 (originally nos. 2822 and 3495), MCCH; Johnson, *The United States Army Invades the New River Valley;* 1870 census; "Enlistment record of Oscar Fractim," Miscellaneous Personal Papers, USCT, fold3.com; Pension record of Othello Fraction, USCT Pensions.

19. Dyer, *A Compendium of the War of the Rebellion,* 1726 and 1730; Pension record of Othello Fraction, USCT Pensions.

20. Hunter, *Bound in Wedlock,* 158–59; Pension application of Othello Fraction, USCT Pensions.

21. Elizabeth Allan Langhorne Payne, "A Brief Outline of My Life for the Benefit of my Grandchildren," Folder 50, Isaac White Papers, Ms 97-013, VT; Janie Milton transcript, Box 1, Folder 38, John Nicolay Papers, Ms 87-027, VT; File of William Moon (sometimes "Moore"), SCCV.

5. FROM SLAVERY TO FREEDOM

1. *Records of the Field Offices for the State of Virginia, Bureau of Refugees, Freedmen, and Abandoned Lands, 1865–1872*, 1–5; Miller, "The Freedmen's Bureau and Reconstruction: An Overview," xiii–xxxii.
2. *Minutes of the Valley Baptist Association Session of 1866, Held at Laurel Ridge Church, Roanoke County, Va., August 17, 18, 19, 20ᵗʰ 1866*, 7–8; Thorp, *Facing Freedom*, 161–83. Some of these churches also closed before 1892, so the number active in any given year was never as high as twenty-two.
3. Schaeffer to Brown, July 25, 1866, and Schaeffer to Sherwood, October 25, 1866, both in BRFAL-FOVA, reel 67; Thorp, *Facing Freedom*, 118–60.
4. MC Cohabitation; Montgomery County Deaths, 1853–1868, MCCH. After the 1843 inventory of James Patton Preston's estate, no record has been found of Mary (b. 1821), Georgi or George (b. 1823), Juda (b. 1827), or Rebecca Fraction (b. 1836).
5. Marriage license of Wilson Capers, Marriage Licenses, 1882: 98, MCCH; 1867 Census (Caperton); U.S. Census 1870 (Capers), and Will of Virginia Capers, Will Book 12: 384, MCCH. She does appear, however, on the 1880 U.S. census as "Virgin" Fraction.
6. Will Book 12: 384, MCCH. There is a stone for Virginia Fraction Capers in the cemetery at Smithfield, but it is modern memorial to commemorate her life and does not mark the actual site of her burial "Smithfield slave descendant to share her heritage," *Roanoke Times*, February 8, 2018.
7. Accounts of William B. Preston, Robert T. Preston, and James F. Preston, Harvey Black Medical Accounts, Box 7, Black-Kent-Apperson Papers, Ms1974-003, VT; MC Cohabitation. Othello Fraction, born in 1845, does not appear on the inventory of James Patton Preston's estate, which was drawn up in 1843, but was born by the time the slaves were actually divided in 1847.
8. The service records of Thomas and Othello Fraction are accessible at "Civil War Service Records, Union Records, Colored Troops," at fold3.com (the originals are in Record Group 94, National Archives, Washington, DC).
9. Ibid.; Pension record of Othello Fraction, USCT Pensions; Schaeffer to Remington, February 14, 1867, BRFAL-FOVA, reel 67; 1865 Census; John

B. Radford to Anne Radford Wharton, n.d., Wharton Family Papers in private possession of Susan Bell (information included in email message to author from William C. Davis, who is editing Gabriel Wharton's wartime letters for publication, April 16, 2019). Dates are sometimes confused in the various sources describing the Fractions' dispute with Robert Preston, but those used in the text seem to be the most accurate.

10. Schaeffer to Remington, February 14, 1867, and February 16, 1867, BRFAL-FOVA, reel 67; Pension record of Othello Fraction, USCT Pensions.

11. The service records of Thomas and Othello Fraction are accessible at "Civil War Service Records, Union Records, Colored Troops," at fold3.com (the originals are in Record Group 94, National Archives, Washington, DC); Schaeffer to Brown, February 25, 1867, BRFAL-FOVA, reel 67; "Colored Members, Blacksburg, 1866" in "Record of Baptisms, 1859–1878," Box 5, Whisner Memorial Methodist Church Records, Ms 64-003, VT.

12. Commonwealth v. Othello Fraction, Criminal A-711, MCCH; Commonwealth v. Thomas Fraction, Criminal A-716, MCCH; Order Book, Cir. Court, no. 4, p. 427, MCCH; March 4, 1867, Order Book, Co. Court Comm. Law & Chancy, 1859–1868, MCCH; Schaeffer to Remington, February 14 and 16, 1867, BRFAL-FOVA, reel 67; Remington's endorsement on Schaeffer's letter of February 14 in Registers of Letters Received and Endorsements, BRFAL-FOVA, reel 195.

13. Charles Schaeffer, the local agent of the Freedmen's Bureau, reported the bail was $100 each; see Schaeffer to Remington, February 16, 1867, BRFAL-FOVA, reel 67. This is confirmed by the magistrate's order granting bail (Judgments 1867, MCCH), though the court order book suggests it was $50 (Order Book Co. Court Comm. Law & Chancery, 1859–1868, March 4, 1867, MCCH).

14. Schaeffer to Remington, February 14, 1867, BRFAL-FOVA, reel 67; Commonwealth v. Othello Fraction, Criminal A-711, MCCH; Commonwealth v. Thomas Fraction, Criminal A-716, MCCH; Order Book, Cir. Court, no. 4, p. 427, MCCH; March 4, 1867, Order Book, Co. Court Comm. Law & Chancy, 1859–1868, MCCH; Schaeffer to Austin, May 6, 1867, BRFAL-FOVA, reel 68; Schaeffer to Mallery, May 25, 1867, BRFAL-FOVA, reel 67.

15. "Poll Book of Colored Voters in . . . County of Montgomery," October 22, 1867, Secretary of the Commonwealth Election Records, Acc. 50706, Record Group 13, LOV; 1867 Census. The enumerator on the 1867 census seems to have used a system of dots to identify children born to couples who had not registered their marriages in 1866. Their failure to register could have been because one of the parents had died or been sold away, because the

couple had chosen not to remain together once slavery ended, or because the mother had never been in a long-term relationship with the father. Mary Fraction, Othello's wife, was twenty-eight years old in 1867 and was identified on the census as Black. Willis, who was marked with a dot on the census, was identified as mulatto, so it is possible that Willis was Mary's son by a White man. Unfortunately, the 1867 census is the only record yet found of Willis Fraction, and his precise identity remains a mystery.

16. "Record of Baptisms, 1859–1878," Box 5, and "Recording Stewards Book, 1859–1880," Box 3, Folder 6, both in Whisner Memorial Methodist Church Records, Ms 64-003, VT; *Christian Recorder,* June 22, 1867; Stowell, *Rebuilding Zion,* 80–99.

17. "Poll Book of Colored Voters in . . . County of Montgomery," October 22, 1867, Secretary of the Commonwealth Election Records, Acc. 50706, Record Group 13, LOV; Schaeffer to "Pay Master Genl.," June 25, 1866, BRFAL-FOVA, reel 67; Wm. Fowler to Oliver Brown, April 6, 1867, logged April 22, 1867, in Letters Received, BRFAL-FOVA, reel 67; Thorp, *Facing Freedom,* 85–87.

18. "Gray's New Map of Salem" (Philadelphia: O.W. Gray and Son, n.d.) The LOV dates its copy of the map to 1878 (755,826 T2 1878 Map Collection), while the Salem Museum, Salem, VA assigns a date of c. 1883 to its copy; Long, *South of Main.*

19. Deposition of Thomas Fraction in Preston v. Preston, Roanoke County Chancery 1886-030 (originally no. 1243), accessed through the LOV's Virginia Memory Site; Pension record of Thomas Fraction, USCT Pensions; U.S. Censuses 1870 and 1880; Deed Book 7: 138, RCCH; "Gray's New Map of Salem"; Long, *South of Main.*

20. "Gray's New Map of Salem"; Deed Book 7: 138, RCCH; Pension record of Thomas Fraction, USCT Pensions; *Roanoke Times,* December 14, 1892; U.S. Censuses 1870 (Roanoke County, VA), 1880 (Roanoke County, VA), and 1900 (Baltimore City, MD); Baltimore City death certificate, Isabella Fraction, D20333, October 5, 1918, MSA.

21. "Gray's New Map of Salem"; Deed Books H: 31, 32, and 168 and P: 346, RCCH; U.S. Censuses 1880 and 1900 (Baltimore, MD); *(Baltimore) Sun,* July 18, 1878 and May 5, 1900; *Woods' Baltimore City Directory,* 1883 and 1885, Internet Archive, https://archive.org; *Baltimore County Union,* November 3, 1883, and August 22, 1903; Pension record of Othello Fraction, USCT Pensions; Holechek, *Baltimore's Two Cross Keys Villages;* "Cross Keys was a village long before the Rouse era," Frederick N. Rasmussen, *Baltimore Sun,* May 31, 2003; "Black Church a home for history

in Ruxton," Frederick N. Rasmussen, *Baltimore Sun,* February 2, 2008; Baltimore City death certificates for "Other Frackson" (B64519, January 1, 1904), Roosevelt Fraction (C27656, November 23, 1909), and Savilla Fraction (D34336, August 15, 1919), MSA.

22. Montgomery and Roanoke County Personal Property Tax Records, LOV; Blacksburg Town Council Minutes, March 12, 1872, Blacksburg Town Hall, Blacksburg, VA.

23. MC Cohabitation; U.S. Censuses 1870, 1880, and 1900; Deed Books H: 235, O: 297, and 34: 340 RCCH; Will Books 1: 578 and 2: 87, RCCH. Ellen and Armistead's surname appears as both Ragland and Raglin in different records, but in drafting their wills, both used Ragland.

24. Chloe Fraction appears on the 1867 census of freedpeople in Montgomery County living with John, Fanny, and Thomas Fraction. On that census she was marked by the enumerator as unmarried but as having had a partner previously. After that, no record has yet been found of anyone named Chloe Fraction. Beginning in 1870, though, records appear of Chloe Shorts, a widow, who had been enslaved by Robert Preston, who moved to Salem about 1871, who lived next door to Thomas Fraction, and who was trusted enough by Fraction to provide evidence in support of his pension application. No surviving document directly links Chloe Shorts to Chloe Fraction, but they seem to be the same person.

25. Marriage licenses of Samuel Shorts and Sarah Braxton (August 26, 1865) and Samuel Shorts and Sarah Monroe (October 20, 1919), RCCH; 1867 Census; U.S. Censuses 1870, 1880, 1900, and 1910; Deed Book I: 15, RCCH; "Gray's New Map of Salem"; Will Book 2: 263, RCCH; Plaques listing those interred, East Hill Cemetery, Salem, VA.

26. U.S. Censuses 1870 and 1880; Lovely v. Lovely, Roanoke County Chancery, 1873-017 (originally no. 629), accessed at the LOV's Virginia Memory Site; Pension record of Oscar Fraction, USCT Pensions.

27. Ibid.; *Cleveland Gazette,* February 27, 1892, and March 17, 1894; "Estate of Oscar Fraction," Pleas Court, Probate Division, Hardin County, Kenton, OH.

28. Montgomery County Personal Property Tax Records, LOV; File of William Moon (sometimes "Moore"), SCCV; MC Cohabitation; Marriage license of Judy Pate, Marriage Licenses, 1872: 93, MCCH; 1867 Census; U.S. Censuses 1870, 1880, and 1900.

29. MC Cohabitation; Montgomery County Personal Property Tax Records, LOV; 1867 Census.

30. U.S. Censuses 1870 and 1880; "J.P. Preston Appraisement," Will Book 7: 130, MCCH and "J.F. Preston Appraisement," Will Book 9: 421, MCCH;

File of William Moon (sometimes "Moore"), SCCV; Marriage Register 1871 and 1874, MCCH.

31. U.S. Census 1880; File of William Moon (sometimes "Moore"), SCCV; Marriage Licenses 1876: 136, MCCH; Kabrich to Board of Supervisors, August 6, 1881, and Account for Frank Moon, May 23, 1882, both in Box 1, Folder 8, Charles Crush Collection, Ms84-180, VT; "List of Voters / Montgomery Co Va.," September 15, 1883, Box 189, William Mahone Papers, David M. Rubenstein Rare Book & Manuscript Library, Duke University.

32. MC Cohabitation; Montgomery County Personal Property Tax Records, LOV; Schaeffer to Austin, June 4, 1867, BRFAL-FOVA, reel 68; 1867 Census; Marriage license for Judy Pate and Ned Vandross, Marriage Licenses, 1872: 93, MCCH.

33. U.S. Censuses 1870, 1880, 1900, 1910, 1920, and 1930; Record of Ellen Moon, "Virginia, Deaths and Burials Index, 1853-1917," Ancestry.com; Conversation with Scott L. Graves, August 1, 2018; Record of Preston Moon, "Virginia, Select Marriages, 1785-1940," Ancestry.com; Record of Lucy Moon, "All Virginia Death Records, 1912-2014," Ancestry.com.

34. MC Cohabitation; 1867 Census; "J.P. Preston Appraisement," Will Book 7: 130, MCCH; "J.F. Preston Appraisement," Will Book 9: 421, MCCH; "Poll Book of Colored Voters in . . . County of Montgomery," October 22, 1867, Secretary of the Commonwealth Election Records, Acc. 50706, Record Group 13, LOV; U.S. Censuses 1870 and 1880; Marriage Licenses, 1870: 5, MCCH.

35. Marsha McNorton Saunders seems to have died by 1865, leaving a widower and four children; see "Interview with Mrs. Nettie Anderson," Box 11, Series 5, Richard B. Dickenson Papers, Ms. 2011-043, VT). No evidence has yet been found of Montreville (b. 1822), Emily (b. 1826), or Nancy McNorton (b. 1833) after their inclusion on the 1843 inventory of James Patton Preston's estate.

36. MC Cohabitation; 1867 Census; Accounts of William Ballard Preston with Harvey Black, James Otey, and Henry Ribble, Adms. of William Ballard Preston v. Heirs of William Ballard Preston, Chancery 1900-014 (originally nos. 2822 and 3495), MCCH.

37. U.S. Census 1870; Thorp, *Facing Freedom*, 195–97; Schaeffer to Mallery, August 25, 1867, BRFAL-FOVA, reel 67.

38. U.S. Censuses 1870, 1880, 1900, and 1910; Deed Book U: 299, MCCH; Pension record of Taylor McNorton, PCW Pensions.

39. Class records, "Register of Christiansburg Station, Roanoke District, Baltimore Conf., M.E. Church, South," St. Paul United Methodist Church, Christiansburg, VA; "Record of Baptisms, 1859-1878," Box 5, Whisner

Memorial Methodist Church Records, Ms 64-003, VT; Thorp, *Facing Freedom*, 166–68; "Petition of Trustees of Methodist Episcopal Church (Colored)," Chancery 1891-001, MCCH.

40. MC Cohabitation; 1867 Census; Deed Book H: 168, RCCH; Mechanics Liens 1887: 125–26, MCCH; Deed Books U:377, 41:113, and 57:353, MCCH; U.S. Censuses 1870, 1880, 1900, 1910, and 1920; Death certificate of Eliza McNorton, "All Virginia Death Records, 1912–2014," Ancestry .com; Account of Nannie Kate McNorton, "United States, Freedman's Bank Records, 1865–1874," familyseatch.org; *Catalogue of the Officers and Students of Shaw University 1886–1887; Catalogue of the Officers and Students of Shaw University 1893–1894.*

41. U.S. Census 1870; Thorp, *Facing Freedom*, 74 and 102–3; Will Book 10: 116, MCCH; Deed Books R: 581; V: 461; W: 422; Z: 472; 39: 111, 456, and 531; 41: 356; and 42: 508, MCCH; Adms. of William Ballard Preston v. Heirs of William Ballard Preston, Chancery 1900-014 (originally nos. 2822 and 3495), MCCH.

42. "Landbooks," MCCH; Montgomery County Personal Property Tax Records, LOV; "Poll Book of Colored Voters in . . . County of Montgomery," October 22, 1867, Secretary of the Commonwealth Election Records, Acc. 50706, Record Group 13, LOV; Thorp, *Facing Freedom*, 212–16; Order Book County Court, No. 3: 220 and 273, MCCH; Deed Books 43: 423 and 455 and 55: 8, MCCH; Hatcher v. McNorton, Chancery 1898-003 (originally no. 1630), MCCH; Stephens v. McNorton, Chancery 1899-009 (originally no. 2388), MCCH; McNorton v. McNorton, Chancery 1906-039 (originally no. 2099), MCCH.

43. Chester McNorton to his parents, April 12, April 25, April 26, December 12, and December 20, 1904, McNorton v. McNorton, Chancery, 1906-039 (originally no. 2099), MCCH; McNorton v. McNorton, Chancery 1911-003 (originally no. 2422), MCCH; Gravestone of Frank McNorton, Schaeffer Community Cemetery, Christiansburg, VA; U.S. Census 1910; Deed Book 37: 352 and 442, FCCH; Death certificate of Orville McNorton, "Ohio Deaths, 1908–1953," familysearch.org.

44. Pension record of Robert McNorton, USCT Pensions; Deed Book H: 168, RCCH; 1870 census; Deed Book T: 239, MCCH; Marriage Licenses 1878: 30, MCCH; Gravestones of Robert and Ellen McNorton, Schaeffer Community Cemetery, Christiansburg, VA.

45. Censuses 1870, 1880, and 1900; Record of Lizzie Fliggins, "All Virginia Death Records, 1912–2014," Ancestry.com.; Will Book 9: 421, MCCH; MC Cohabitation; 1867 Census; Gravestone of Eliza Burks in Schaeffer Community Cemetery, Christiansburg, VA.

46. MC Cohabitation; 1867 Census; censuses of 1870, 1880, 1900, 1910, 1920, and 1930; Harrison, *A Consecrated Life*, 310; Gravestone of William H. Poindexter in Schaeffer Community Cemetery, Christiansburg, VA; Marriage Licenses, 1905: 154, MCCH; Records of James Taylor, Peter Fliggins, and Elizabeth Fliggins, "All Virginia Death Records, 1912–2014," Ancestry.com.; Gravestone of William B. Smith in Schaeffer Community Cemetery, Christiansburg, VA.

47. 1867 Census; U.S. Censuses 1870, 1880, 1900, 1910, 1920, and 1930; Marriage Licenses, 1871: 26, MCCH; Record of Grace Strothers, "Ohio Deaths, 1908–1953," familysearch.org.

48. 1867 Census; U.S. Censuses 1870, 1880, and 1900; Record of Grace McNorton, "All West Virginia, Deaths Index, 1853–1873," Ancestry.com.

6. OUTWARD AND UPWARD

1. U.S. Censuses 1870, 1880, 1900, and 1910.

2. Smith, "Virginia During Reconstruction"; Wynes, *Race Relations in Virginia*; Maddex, *The Virginia Conservatives*; Dailey, *Before Jim Crow*; Thorp, *Facing Freedom*.

3. Thorp, *Facing Freedom*, 27–29 and 70–117.

4. U.S. Censuses 1880 and 1900; Record of Robert C. McNorton, "WWI Draft Registration Cards," fold3.com; *Catalogue of the Officers and Students of Shaw University, 1891–1892*, 13; Shaw University, Raleigh. *Twenty-First Annual Catalog of the Officers and Students . . . 1894–1895*, 48; *Druggists' Circular and Chemical Gazette*, vol. 41 (1897), 326; "Negro Patriotism," *Colored American*, March 12, 1898; "A Roster of the 6th Virginia Volunteer Infantry," http://www.spanamwar.com/6thVAroster.html.

5. Gatewood, "Virginia's Negro Regiment in the Spanish American War."

6. Ibid.

7. Record of Robert C. McNorton, "All Georgia, Marriage Records from Select Counties, 1828–1978," Ancestry.com; Record of Robert C. McNorton, "U.S. Army, Register of Enlistments, 1798–1914," Ancestry.com; Russell, "I Feel Sorry for These People"; Report of commissioner for R. C. McNorton, Fiduciary Settlement Book, 2: 561, MCCH; Records of Robert C. McNorton and Lou Ella McNorton, "Virginia, Death Records, 1912–2014," Ancestry.com; *Annual Report of the Superintendent of Public Education in the Commonwealth of Virginia . . . 1914–15*, 182; *Roanoke Times*, May 12, 1918; *Fifty-Fifth Annual Catalog* [of the Hampton Normal and Agricultural Institute].

8. Lewis, *Black Coal Miners in America*, 121–42; Trotter, *Coal, Class, and Color*, 9–38; Fain, *Black Huntington*, 22–44; Thorp, *Facing Freedom*, 27–32.

9. U.S. Censuses 1880, 1900, 1910, and 1920; *(Indianapolis) Freeman,* May 12, 1900; Deed Book 6: 644, RCCH; *The Alumni Journal of the Virginia Normal and Collegiate Institute,* 21; Record of Saunders B. Moon, "West Virginia, Marriages Index, 1785–1971," Ancestry.com; Obituary of Olga Ellen Moon Hall, *Bluefield Daily Telegraph,* July 11, 1991.

10. U.S. Censuses 1900, 1910, and 1920; Kate McNorton, Marriage Licenses, 1879: 62, MCCH; Record of Ethel McNorton, "New Jersey, Marriage Records, 1670–1965," Ancestry.com; Records of Ethel McNorton and Florence McNorton, Register of Marriages, 1889–1903: 184–85, FCCH; R. E. Peters, Will Book 2: 155, Raleigh County Courthouse, Beckley, WV; Kimberly Walker, "WVU journalism professor extends project exploring race issues in southern W.Va.," February 13, 2014, http://wvutoday.wvu .edu/n/2014/02/13/wvu-journalism-professor-extends-project-exploring -race-issues-in-southern-wv; Florence Price, Fayette County Deaths, vol. 1: 116, FCCH; Record of Delphia Moon, "Virginia, Select Marriages, 1785–1940," Ancestry.com.

11. Stanley McNorton, Register of Marriages, 1889–1903: 166, FCCH; "Colored Candidate," *Raleigh Register,* March 12, 1908; Arter, *Echoes from a Pioneer Life,* 46; Chester McNorton to "Dear Mother and Father," December 12, 1904, McNorton v. McNorton, Chancery, 1906-039 (formerly no. 2099), MCCH; Camarena and Brown, *Historic Structure Report . . . Bank of Glen Jean,* 226–34; Deed of trust by Stanley McNorton, Trust Deeds, Book K: 124, FCCH; "On the Yards," *Dallas Morning News,* Oct, 14, 1903.

12. U.S. Censuses 1900 and 1910; Arter, *Echoes from a Pioneer Life,* 46 and 54; "Colored Candidate," *Raleigh Register,* March 12, 1908; Fain, "Race, River, and the Railroad," 290.

13. Trust Deeds, Books J:508 and K:124, FCCH; Deed Book 37: 52, FCCH; Record of Howard S. McNorton, "WWI Draft Registration Cards," fold3 .com; U.S. Censuses 1920 and 1930; Record of Stanley McNorton, "Ohio Deaths, 1908–1953," familysearch.org; *Washington Bee,* April 3, 1920.

14. U.S. Censuses 1880, 1900, 1910, 1920, and 1940; Baltimore City death certificates for Roosevelt Fraction (C27656, November 23, 1909), Mary E. Diggs (G42625, August 1, 1946), and Frank Fraction (G72976, March 30, 1949), MSA; *(Baltimore) Sun,* February 17, 1897; Personal communication Kerri Moseley-Hobbs.

15. U.S. Censuses 1880, 1900, and 1910; Marriage Licenses, 1874: 3, MCCH; Record of Jacob Hickman, "Ohio, Births and Christenings Index, 1774– 1973," Ancestry.com; "Rendville" in Ohio History Central, https:// ohiohistorycentral.org/w/Rendville,_Ohio; Iowa state censuses of 1885,

1895, 1905, and 1915, Ancestry.com; Schweider, Hraba, and Schweider, *Buxton;* Stek, "Muchakinock."

16. U.S. Censuses 1870, 1880, 1900, 1910, 1920, and 1930; Red River County tax roll, 1884, "Texas, County Tax Rolls, 1837–1910," familysearch.org; Record of H. F. McNorton "Texas, Select County Marriages, 1837–2015," Ancestry.com; *American Baptist Year-Book 1890*, 168; "Colored Normal," *Dallas Morning News,* July 16, 1895; "A Good Showing," *Topeka Plaindealer,* January 27, 1905; "Teachers Assigned to Their Schools," *Dallas Morning News,* August 23, 1914; Email message to author from Ruth Hatcher, May 1, 2019; Death certificates for Hugh Fleming McNorton (June 26, 1935) and Laura McNorton (January 11, 1935), "Ohio Deaths, 1908–1953," familysearch.org.

17. U.S. Censuses 1880, 1900, 1910, and 1920; *Catalogue of the Officers and Students of Shaw University, 1886–1887,* 9; *Catalogue of the Officers and Students of Shaw University, 1889–1890,* 12; *Catalogue of the Officers and Students of Shaw University, 1891–1892,* 16; "Death or Marriage," *Birmingham Age,* August 11, 1895; "The Local Courts," *Dallas Morning News,* November 21, 1895; Record of C. M. McNorton, "Texas, Convict and Conduct Registers, 1875–1945," Ancestry.com; Record of C. M. McNorton, "Texas, Select County Marriage Index, 1837–1965," Ancestry.com; *Santa Barbara [1909–10] City Directory,* "U.S. City Directories, 1822–1995," Ancestry.com; Record of Charles McNorton, "California Death Index, 1905–1939," Ancestry.com; Record of Lena McNorton, "California Death Index, 1940–1997," Ancestry.com.

18. U.S. Censuses 1900, 1910, 1920, 1930, and 1940; Marriage Register, 1861–1921, Pittsylvania County Courthouse, Chatham, VA; Record of Hattie Dabney Woods, "North Carolina Deaths and Burials, 1898–1994," familysearch.org; Record of James McNorton, "WWI Draft Registration Cards," fold3.com.

19. U.S. Censuses 1900, 1910, 1920, 1930, and 1940; Record of Minor McNorton, "WWI Draft Registration Cards," fold3.com.; Record of Minor McNorton, "Railroad Retirement Pension Index, 1934–1987," Ancestry.com; note from Simon McNorton posted on People of Color in Old Tennessee, http://www.tngenweb.org/tncolor/queries/cqry5-00.htm.

20. Record of Augustine O. McNorton, "Ohio Deaths, 1908–1953," familysearch.org; Harrison, *A Consecrated Life,* 325; Raymond Hylton, "University History," https://www.vuu.edu/about-vuu/history; "Union University Had Good Session," (Richmond) *Times,* May 23, 1901; United States Patents US727185A and US739904, patents.google.com; "Railroad Invention by a Colored Man," *Richmond Planet,* December 6, 1902; "A

Catholic Student Writes," *Topeka Plaindealer,* June 10, 1904; *New York Age,* February 2, 1905; "For Colored Catholics," *(Richmond) Reformer,* January 28, 1908.

21. *Nashville Directory,* 1914, "U.S. City Directories, 1822-1995," Ancestry .com; *Meharry News,* 56; U.S. Census 1920; Record of Mary McNorton, "Illinois, Deaths and Stillbirths Index, 1916-1947," Ancestry.com; Record of Augustine J. O. McNorton, "United States Deceased Physician File (AMA), 1864-1968," familysearch.org.; Record of Augustine O. McNorton, "Ohio Deaths, 1908-1953," familysearch.org.

22. "Population of Montana by Counties and Minor Civil Divisions," *Census Bulletin* 33, January 17, 1901; Fullerton Collection.

23. Malone, *The Battle for Butte,* 24-33; "Shaffer's Chapel African Methodist Episcopal Church," https://www.nps.gov/places/shaffer-s-chapel-african -methodist-episcopal-church.htm; *Butte Daily Post,* June 2, 1887; *Weekly Montanian,* October 12, 1895; Land patent of William McNorton, U.S. Department of the Interior, Bureau of Land Management, General Land Office, https://glorecords.blm.gov/default.aspx, Accession Nr. MTMTAA 067426; Fullerton Collection; *Sanders County Ledger,* September 2, 1910.

24. Fullerton Collection; Record of William McNorton, "Montana, County Marriages, 1865-1950," familysearch.org.

25. William McNorton to ??, February 3, 1909, quoted in *Sanders County Ledger,* February 12, 1909; Marriage Licenses, 1909: 8, MCCH; U.S. Censuses 1900 and 1910; Fullerton Collection; *Sanders County Ledger,* August 5, 1910, and January 28, 1916.

26. *Sanders County Ledger,* August 3, 1906, August 16, 1907, September 2, 1910, May 9, 1913, and April 19, 1917; *Anaconda (MT) Standard,* June 15, 1911; Fullerton Collection.

27. *Sanders County Independent Ledger,* September 9, 1931, February 8, 1933, May 4, 1938, and July 20, 1938; Fullerton Collection.

28. U.S. Census 1880; "This Land is Our Land," *Evansville Living,* July/ August 2018, http://www.evansvilleliving.com/articles/our-land; Record of Chester McNorton, "U.S. Army, Register of Enlistments, 1798-1914," Ancestry.com; Stewart, *American Military History,* 304.

29. Chester McNorton's record of enlistments and service is drawn from the "U.S. Army, Register of Enlistments, 1798-1914" and "U.S. Returns from Regular Army Infantry Regiments, 1821-1916," Ancestry.com.

30. Nankivell, *History of the Twenty-Fifth Regiment United States Infantry,* 42-64 (quotation on 44); Record of Chester McNorton, "U.S. Returns from Regular Army Infantry Regiments, 1821-1916," Ancestry.com.

31. Nankivell, *History of the Twenty-Fifth Regiment*, 60–62.

32. Ibid., 65–85; Gatewood, *"Smoked Yankees"* (quotations on 41 and 45).

33. Linn, *The Philippine War*, 3–64; Silbey, *A War of Frontier and Empire*, 3–78; Gatewood, *"Smoked Yankees,"* 239–45.

34. Nankivell, *History of the Twenty-Fifth Regiment*, 85–113 (quotation on 88); Gatewood, "Black Americans and the Quest for Empire" (quotation on 558); *Washington Bee*, June 24, 1899; Michael Robinson to the *Colored American*, c. February 1, 1900, printed in Gatewood, *"Smoked Yankees,"* 264–68.

35. Records of Chester McNorton in "U.S. Army, Register of Enlistments, 1798–1914" and "U.S. Returns from Regular Army Infantry Regiments, 1821–1916," Ancestry.com; Nankivell, *History of the Twenty-Fifth Regiment*, 94–97.

36. Deed Book 49: 55, MCCH; Chester McNorton to "Dear Mother & Father," April 12, 1904, and Chester McNorton to "Dear Father," April 26, 1904, both in McNorton v. McNorton, Chancery 1906-039 (originally no. 2099), MCCH.

37. Chester McNorton to "Dear Mother & Father," April 12, 1904, McNorton v. McNorton, Chancery 1906-039 (originally no. 2099, MCCH); Register of Marriages 1904–1909: 115, FCCV.

38. U.S. Censuses 1910, 1930, and 1940; *Sanders County Ledger*, October 13, 1905; *Daily Missoulian*, June 25, 1910, June 19, 1913, July 15, 1914, and July 29, 1917; Record of Chester McNorton, "Montana, County Marriages, 1865–1987," Ancestry.com; Record of Lillie McNorton, "Montana, State Deaths, 1907–2016," Ancestry.com; Record of Chester McNorton, "Washington, Select Death Certificates, 1907–1960," Ancestry.com.

39. U.S. Census 1880; (*Phoenix*) *Republican Herald*, February 22, 1890; *Missoulian*, October 13, 1900; *Helena Independent*, November 15, 1900.

40. *Sanders County Ledger*, June 7, 1907; Land patent of Burman McNorton, U.S. Department of the Interior, Bureau of Land Management, General Land Office, https://glorecords.blm.gov/default.aspx, Accession Nr. MV-0747-137; Burman McNorton's record of enlistment and service is drawn from "U.S. Army, Register of Enlistments, 1798–1914" and "U.S. Returns from Regular Army Infantry Regiments, 1821–1916," Ancestry.com.; censuses of 1920, 1930, and 1940; Toledo City Directories, 1913–19, in "U.S. City Directories, 1822–1995," Ancestry.com; Record of Burman McNorton, "Ohio, County Marriage Records, 1774–1993," Ancestry.com; Record of Burman McNorton, "Michigan Marriages, 1868–1926," familysearch.org; Record of Burman McNorton, "Ohio Deaths, 1908–1953," familysearch.org.

41. *Sanders County Ledger*, July 30 and August 20, 1909; "Descriptive List of the Convict" in Montana State Prison Records, 1869–1974, Montana Memory

Project; U.S. census 1920; Email message to author from Elliott Mason, October 29, 2019; Record of Hugh McNorton, "West Virginia Deaths, 1804–1999," familysearch.org.

CONCLUSION

1. "Record of Baptisms, 1869–1878," Box 5, Whisner Memorial Methodist Church Records, Ms 64-003, VT.

❖ BIBLIOGRAPHY ❖

ARCHIVAL COLLECTIONS

Blacksburg Presbyterian Church, Blacksburg, VA
    Records of the Session of the Blacksburg Church
Christiansburg Presbyterian Church, Christiansburg, VA
    Records of the Church Session, 1827–1869
Duke University, David M. Rubenstein Rare Book & Manuscript Library,
    Durham, NC
    William Mahone Papers
Fayette County Courthouse, Fayetteville, WV
    Deaths
    Deeds
    Register of Marriages
    Trust Deeds
Filson Historical Society, Louisville, KY
    Preston Family Papers
Hardin County Courthouse, Kenton, OH
    Probate
Historic Smithfield, Blacksburg, VA
History Museum of Western Virginia, Roanoke
    Breckinridge Collection
Library of Congress, Washington, DC
    Preston Family of Virginia Papers
Library of Virginia, Richmond, VA
    Department of Taxation, Personal Property Tax Books
    Montgomery County, Miscellaneous Court Records, 1750–1861
    Secretary of the Commonwealth Election Records

Maryland State Archives, Annapolis, MD
    Death Certificates
Montana Historical Society, Helena, MT
    Neil Fullerton Research Collection
Montgomery County Courthouse, Christiansburg, VA
    Book of Free Negroes
    Cohabitation Register
    Common Law
    Court of Chancery
    Criminal Papers
    Deaths
    Deed Books
    Fiduciary Settlements
    Marriage Licenses
    Marriage Registers
    Mechanics' Liens
    Land Books
    Order Books
    Will Books
    Wills
National Archives, Washington, DC
    Civil War and Later Pension Files, Department of Veterans Affairs
        (RG 15)
    Federal Military Pension Application—Pre–Civil War (RG 15)
    Pension and bounty land application files based upon service prior
        to the Civil War, Records of the Veterans Administration
        (RG 15)
    Records of the Bureau of Land Management (RG 49)
    Records of the Bureau of Refugees, Freedmen, and Abandoned
        Lands (RG 105)
    Southern Claims Commission—allowed (RG 217) and disallowed
        (RG 233)
    U.S. Census, 1810
    U.S. Census, 1820
    U.S. Census, 1830
    U.S. Census, 1840
    U.S. Census, 1850, Population, Slave, and Agriculture Schedules
    U.S. Census, 1860, Population, Slave, and Agriculture Schedules
    U.S. Census, 1870, Population and Agriculture Schedules

U.S. Census, 1880, Population and Agriculture Schedules
U.S. Census, 1900, Population Schedule
U.S. Census, 1910, Population Schedule
U.S. Census, 1920, Population Schedule
U.S. Census, 1930, Population Schedule
U.S. Census, 1940, Population Schedule
Office of the Town Manager, Blacksburg, VA
    Council Minutes
Pittsylvania County Courthouse, Chatham, VA
    Marriage Register
Raleigh County Courthouse, Beckley, WV
    Wills
Roanoke County Courthouse, Salem, VA
    Deeds
    Marriage Licenses
    Wills
St. Paul United Methodist Church, Christiansburg, VA
    Records of Quarterly Meetings
    Register of the Christiansburg Station
Salem Museum, Salem, VA
University of Virginia, Small Special Collections, Charlottesville, VA
    John Quincy Adams Buford Papers, 1844–1865
Virginia Historical Society, Richmond, VA
    Caperton Family Papers, 1729–1973
    Preston Family Papers, 1773–1862
Virginia Tech, Newman Library, Special Collections, Blacksburg, VA
    Black-Kent-Apperson Papers
    Charles W. Crush Collection
    Richard B. Dickenson Papers
    William E. Hoge Family Papers
    John Nicolay Papers
    Smithfield Preston Foundation Papers
    Whisner Memorial Methodist Church Records
    Isaac White Papers

ONLINE DATABASES

Ancestry.com
    All Georgia, Marriage Records from Select Counties, 1828–1978

All Virginia Death Records, 1912–2014
All West Virginia, Deaths Index, 1853–1873
California Death Index, 1905–1939
California Death Index, 1940–1997
Illinois, Deaths and Stillbirths Index, 1916–1947
Iowa State Censuses
Montana, State Deaths, 1907–2016
New Jersey, Marriage Records, 1670–1965
Ohio, Births and Christenings Index, 1774–1973
Ohio, County Marriage Records, 1774–1993
Railroad Retirement Pension Index, 1934–1987
Texas, Convict and Conduct Registers, 1875–1945
Texas, Select County Marriages, 1837–2015
U.S. Army, Register of Enlistments, 1798–1914
U.S. City Directories, 1822–1995
U.S. Returns from Regular Army Infantry Regiments, 1821–1916
Virginia, Deaths and Burials Index, 1853–1917
Virginia, Select Marriages, 1785–1940
Washington, Select Death Certificates, 1907–1960
West Virginia, Marriages Index, 1785–1971
Familysearch.org
Michigan Marriages, 1868–1926
Montana, County Marriages, 1865–1950
North Carolina Deaths and Burials, 1898–1994
Ohio Deaths, 1908–1953
United States Deceased Physician File (AMA), 1864–1968
United States, Freedman's Bank Records, 1865–1874
Texas, County Tax Rolls, 1837–1910
West Virginia Deaths, 1804–1999
Fold3.com
Civil War Service Records, Union Records, Colored Troops
Miscellaneous Personal Papers, USCT
WWI Draft Registration Cards
General Land Office Records (https://glorecords.blm.gov/default.aspx)
Montana Memory Project (https://mtmemory.org/digital/custom/home/#/)
Trans-Atlantic Slave Trade Database (https://www.slavevoyages.org/voyage
/database)
Virginia Landmarks Register (https://www.dhr.virginia.gov/historic
-registers/)
Virginia Memory (https://www.virginiamemory.com)

NEWSPAPERS AND MAGAZINES

Anaconda (MT) Standard
Beckley (WVA) Post-Herald
Baltimore County (MD) Union
Baltimore (MD) Sun
Birmingham (AL) Age
Bluefield (WVA) Daily Telegraph
Butte (MT) Daily Post
Christian Recorder (Nashville, TN)
Cleveland (OH) Gazette
Colored American (New York)
Daily Missoulian (Missoula, MT)
Dallas (TX) Morning News
Druggists' Circular and Chemical Gazette (New York)
Evansville (IL) Living
Freeman (Indianapolis, IN)
Helena (MT) Independent
Maryland Gazette (Annapolis)
Messenger (Christiansburg, VA)
Missoulian (Missoula, MT)
New Star (Christiansburg, VA)
New York Age
Raleigh Register (Beckley, WVA)
Reformer (Richmond, VA)
Republican Herald (Phoenix, AZ)
Richmond (VA) Planet
Roanoke (VA) Times
Sanders County Ledger (Thompson Falls, MT)
Times (Richmond, VA)
Topeka (KS) Plaindealer
Washington (DC) Bee
Weekly Montanian (Thompson Falls, MT)

BOOKS, ARTICLES, AND DISSERTATIONS

Acts of the General Assembly of the State of Virginia Passed at Called Session, 1862.
    Richmond: William F. Ritchie, 1862.
Alumni Journal of the Virginia Normal and Collegiate Institute. Petersburg:
    Kirkham & Co., 1898.

American Baptist Year-Book 1890. Philadelphia: American Baptist Publication Society, n.d.

Annual Report of the Superintendent of Public Education in the Commonwealth of Virginia . . . 1914–15. Richmond: Davis Bottom, Superintendent of Education, 1917.

Arnesen, Eric. *Brotherhoods of Color: Black Railroad Workers and the Struggle for Equality.* Cambridge, MA: Harvard University Press, 2001.

Arter, Jared M. *Echoes from a Pioneer Life.* Atlanta: A.B. Caldwell Publishing, 1922.

Azaare, Christopher Anabila. "Sacred Trees in Ghana." Transcribed and introduced by Anatoli Ignatov. *Cold Mountain Review* 45 (Fall 2016). https://www.coldmountainreview.org/issues/fall-2016-special-issue-on-forests/sacred-trees-in-ghana-by-christopher-anabila-azaare.

Bergstrom, Peter V. "Nothing So Certain: Taxes in Colonial Virginia." Colonial Williamsburg Foundation, Department of Historical Research, 1984. https://research.colonialwilliamsburg.org/DigitalLibrary/view/index.cfm?doc=ResearchReports%5CRR0127.xml&highlight=.

Berlin, Ira. *Slaves Without Masters: The Free Negro in the Antebellum South.* New York: Vintage Books, 1974.

Billings, Warren M. "The Law of Servants and Slaves in Seventeenth-Century Virginia." *Virginia Magazine of History and Biography* 99 (1991): 45–62.

Bongmba, Elias Kifon, ed. *The Wiley-Blackwell Companion to African Religions.* Oxford: John Wiley & Sons, 2012.

Brewer, James H. *The Confederate Negro: Virginia's Craftsmen and Military Laborers, 1861–1865.* Durham, NC: Duke University Press, 1969.

Bruce, Philip Alexander, Lyon Gardner Tyler, and Richard Lee Morton, *History of Virginia,* Chicago and New York: American Historical Society, 1924.

Burton, Orville Vernon. *In My Father's House Are Many Mansions: Family and Community in Edgefield, South Carolina.* Chapel Hill: University of North Carolina Press, 1985.

Camarena, Norma and Sharon A. Brown. *Historic Structure Report: Administrative Data, Historical Data, Architectural Data: Bank of Glen Jean, New River Gorge National River, West Virginia.* U.S. Department of the Interior, National Park Service, 1990.

Catalogue of the Officers and Students of Shaw University 1886–1887. Raleigh, NC: Edwards, Broughton & Co., 1887.

Catalogue of the Officers and Students of Shaw University, 1889–1890. Raleigh, NC: Shaw University Printing Department, 1890.

Catalogue of the Officers and Students of Shaw University, 1891–1892. Raleigh, NC: Shaw University Printing Department, 1892.

Catalogue of the Officers and Students of Shaw University 1893–1894. Raleigh, NC: Shaw University Printing Department, 1894.

Craven, Wesley Frank. *White, Red, and Black: The Seventeenth-Century Virginian*. New York: Norton Library, 1977.

Dailey, Jane. *Before Jim Crow: The Politics of Race in Postemancipation Virginia*. Chapel Hill: University of North Carolina Press, 2000.

Dew, Charles B. *Bond of Iron: Master and Slave at Buffalo Forge*. New York: W. W. Norton & Company, 1994.

Donald, Christopher Ross. "Blacksburg Methodist Churches: Blacksburg Methodist Episcopal Church, South and the Beginnings of St. Paul African Methodist Episcopal Church." A lecture delivered April 16, 2005. http://www.joepayne.org/MethodisminBlacksburg.pdf.

Dunaway, Wilma A. *The African American Family in Slavery and Emancipation*. Cambridge: Cambridge University Press, 2003.

Duncan, Richard R. *Lee's Endangered Left: The Civil War in Western Virginia, Spring of 1864*. Baton Rouge: Louisiana State University Press, 1998.

Dyer, Frederick H. *A Compendium of the War of the Rebellion*. Des Moines: Dyer Publishing Co., 1908.

Ely, Melvin Patrick. *Israel on the Appomattox: A Southern Experiment in Black Freedom from the 1790s Through the Civil War*. New York: Alfred A. Knopf, 2004.

Encyclopedia Virginia. Charlottesville: Virginia Humanities. https://encyclopediavirginia.org.

Eslinger, Ellen. "Free Black Residency in Two Antebellum Counties: How the Laws Functioned." *Journal of Southern History* 79 (2013): 261–98.

Escott, Paul D. *Slavery Remembered: A Record of Twentieth Century Slave Narratives*. Chapel Hill: University of North Carolina Press, 1979.

"This Land is Our Land." *Evansville Living* (July/August 2018). http://www.evansvilleliving.com/articles/our-land.

Fain, Cicero N., III. *Black Huntington: An Appalachian Story*. Urbana: University of Illinois Press, 2019.

———. "Race, River, and the Railroad: Black Huntington, West Virginia, 1871–1929." PhD diss., Ohio State University, 2009.

Fifty-Fifth Annual Catalog. Hampton, VA: The Press of the Hampton Normal and Agricultural Institute, 1922.

Gatewood, Willard B., Jr. "Black Americans and the Quest for Empire." *Journal of Southern History* 38 (1972): 545–66.

———. "Smoked Yankees" and the Struggle for Empire: Letters from Negro Soldiers, 1898–1902. Urbana: University of Illinois Press, 1971.

———. "Virginia's Negro Regiment in the Spanish American War: The Sixth Virginia Volunteers." Virginia Magazine of History and Biography 80 (1971): 193–209.

Genovese, Eugene D. Roll, Jordan, Roll: The World the Slaves Made. New York; Pantheon Books, 1972.

Glanville, Jim. "William Preston the Surveyor and the Great Virginia Land Grab." Smithfield Review 17 (2013): 43–74.

Grimsley, Mark. And Keep Moving On: The Virginia Campaign, May–June 1864. Lincoln: University of Nebraska Press, 2002.

Gutman, Herbert G. The Black Family in Slavery and Freedom, 1750–1925. New York: Pantheon Books, 1976.

Harrison, Charles H. The Story of a Consecrated Life. Philadelphia: J.B. Lippincott Company, 1903.

Hartley, Chris J. Stoneman's Raid: 1865. Winston-Salem, NC: John F. Blair, 2010.

Heinegg, Paul. Free African Americans of North Carolina, Virginia, and South Carolina from the colonial period to about 1820. Baltimore, MD: Clearfield, 2001.

Herndon, G. Melvin. "Hemp in Colonial Virginia." Agricultural History 37, no. 2 (1963): 86–93.

Holechek, Jim. Baltimore's Two Cross Keys Villages: One Black. One White. Lincoln, NE: iUniverse, 2004.

Holmberg, James J., ed. Dear Brother: Letters of William Clark to Johnathan Clark. New Haven and London: Yale University Press, 2002.

Hunter, Tera W. Bound in Wedlock: Slave and Free Black Marriage in the Nineteenth Century. Cambridge, MA: Belknap Press of Harvard University Press, 2017.

Isaac, Rhys. The Transformation of Virginia, 1740–1790. Chapel Hill: University of North Carolina Press, 1982.

Johnson, Patricia Givens. The United States Army Invades the New River Valley, May 1864. Christiansburg, VA: Walpa Publishing, 1986.

Klein, Herbert S. The Atlantic Slave Trade. Cambridge: Cambridge University Press, 1999.

Kornweibel, Theodore, Jr. Railroads in the African American Experience: A Photographic Journey. Baltimore, MD: Johns Hopkins University Press, 2010.

Levin, Kevin M. Searching for Black Confederates: The Civil War's Most Persistent Myth. Chapel Hill: University of North Carolina Press, 2019.

Levine, Bruce. Confederate Emancipation: Southern Plans to Free and Arm Slaves During the Civil War. New York: Oxford University Press, 2006.

Lewis, Ronald L. *Black Coal Miners in America: Race, Class, and Community Conflict, 1780–1980.* Lexington: University Press of Kentucky, 1987.

Lindon, Mary Elizabeth, ed. *Virginia's Montgomery County.* Christiansburg, VA.; Montgomery Museum and Lewis Miller Regional Art Center, 2009.

Linn, Brian McAllister. *The Philippine War, 1899–1902.* Lawrence: University of Kansas Press, 2000.

Long, John D. *South of Main: A History of the Water Street Community of Salem, Virginia.* Salem, VA: Salem Museum & Historical Society, 2000.

Loveland, Anne C. *Southern Evangelicals and the Social Order, 1800–1860.* Baton Rouge and London: Louisiana State University Press, 1980.

Luke, Bob, and John David Smith. *Soldiering for Freedom: How the Union Army Recruited, Trained, and Deployed the U.S. Colored Troops.* Baltimore, MD: Johns Hopkins University Press, 2014.

Maddex, Jack P., Jr. *The Virginia Conservatives, 1867–1879: A Study in Reconstruction Politics.* Chapel Hill: University of North Carolina Press, 1970.

Malone, Michael P. *The Battle for Butte: Mining and Politics on the Northern Frontier, 1864–1906.* Seattle: University of Washington Press, 1981. Reissued in 2006 with a new Foreword.

Manfra, Jo Ann, and Robert R. Dykstra. "Serial Marriage and the Origins of the Black Stepfamily: The Rowanty Evidence." *Journal of American History* 72 (1985): 18–44.

Martinez, Jaime Amanda. *Confederate Slave Impressment in the Upper South.* Chapel Hill: University of North Carolina Press, 2013.

Mathews, Donald G. *Slavery and Methodism: A Chapter in American Morality, 1780–1845.* Princeton, NJ: Princeton University Press, 1965.

McCleskey, Turk. *The Road to Black Ned's Forge: A Story of Race, Sex, and Trade on the Colonial American Frontier.* Charlottesville: University of Virginia Press, 2014.

McMullen, Glenn L., ed. *A Surgeon with Stonewall Jackson; The Civil War Letters of Dr. Harvey Black.* Baltimore, MD: Butternut and Blue, 1995.

The Meharry News: Meharry Medical, Dental and Pharmaceutical Colleges. Catalog of 1917–1918—Announcement for 1918–1919. Nashville, TN: Meharry Medical College, 1918.

Miller, Randall M. "Slaves and Southern Catholicism." In *Masters and Slaves in the House of the Lord,* edited by John Boles 127–52. Lexington: University Press of Kentucky, 1988.

———. "The Freedmen's Bureau and Reconstruction: An Overview." In *The Freedmen's Bureau and Reconstruction: Reconsiderations,* edited by Paul A. Cimbala and Randall M. Miller, xiii–xxxii. New York: Fordham University Press, 1999.

Minutes of the Valley Baptist Association Session of 1866, Held at Laurel Ridge Church, Roanoke County, Va., August 17, 18, 19, 20th 1866. Lynchburg: Virginian Book and Job Office, 1866.

Mitchell, Robert D. *Commercialism and Frontier: Perspectives on the Early Shenandoah Valley.* Charlottesville: University Press of Virginia, 1977.

Moche, Joanne Spiers. *Families of Grace through 1900: Remembering Radford.* Westminster, MD: Heritage Books, 2008.

Morgan, Edmund S. *American Slavery, American Freedom: The Ordeal of Colonial America.* New York: W. W. Norton, 1975.

Nankivell, John H. *History of the Twenty-Fifth Regiment United States Infantry, 1869–1926.* Denver: Smith-Brooks Printing Company, 1927. Reprinted in 1969 by Negro Universities Press.

Nelson, Bernard H. "Confederate Slave Impressment Legislation, 1861–1865." *Journal of Negro History* 31 (1946): 392–410.

Nelson, Lynn A. *Pharsalia: An Environmental Biography of a Southern Plantation, 1780–1880.* Athens: University of Georgia Press, 2007.

Noe, Kenneth W. *Southwest Virginia's Railroad: Modernization and the Sectional Crisis.* Urbana: University of Illinois Press, 1994.

Osborn, Richard. "William Preston: Origins of a Backcountry Political Career." *Journal of Backcountry Studies* 2, no. 2 (2007): 1–10.

———. "William Preston, 1727–1783: The Making of a Frontier Elite." PhD diss., University of Maryland, 1990.

Owen, Christopher H. "By Design: The Social Meaning of Methodist Church Architecture in Nineteenth-Century Georgia." *Georgia Historical Quarterly* 75 (1991): 221–53.

Pargas, Damian Allen. *The Quarters and the Fields: Slave Families in the Non-Cotton South.* Tallahassee: University Press of Florida, 2010.

———. "'Various Means of Providing for Their Own Tables': Comparing Slave Family Economies in the Antebellum South." *American Nineteenth Century History* 7 (2006): 361–87.

Perdue, Charles L., Thomas E. Barden, and Robert K. Phillips, eds., *Weevils in the Wheat: Interviews with Virginia Ex-Slaves.* Charlottesville: University Press of Virginia, 1976.

"Population of Montana by Counties and Minor Civil Divisions." *Census Bulletin* 33, January 17, 1901. Washington, DC: United States Census Office.

Pulice, Michael J. "The Log Outbuilding at Solitude: An Architectural and Archaeological Investigation of Virginia Tech's Second Oldest Building." Master's thesis, Virginia Tech, 2000.

Raboteau, Albert J. *Canaan Land: A Religious History of African Americans.* Oxford and New York: Oxford University Press, 1999.

Records of the Field Offices for the State of Virginia, Bureau of Refugees, Freedmen, and Abandoned Lands, 1865–1872. Washington, DC: United States Congress and National Archives and Records Administration, 2006.

Rediker, Marcus. *The Slave Ship: A Human History.* New York: Viking, 2007.

Revised Code of the Laws of Virginia. Richmond: Thomas Ritchie, 1819.

Richey, Russell E., Kenneth E. Rowe, and Jeanne Miller Schmidt. *The Methodist Experience in America: A History.* Vol. 1. Nashville, TN: Abingdon Press, 2010.

Russell, John Henderson. *The Free Negro in Virginia, 1619–1865.* Baltimore, MD: The Johns Hopkins University Press, 1913.

Russell, Timothy D. "'I Feel Sorry for These People': African American Soldiers in the Philippine-American War, 1899–1902." *Journal of African American History* 99 (2014): 197–222.

Rutman, Darrett B. and Anita H. Rutman. *A Place in Time: Middlesex County, Virginia, 1650–1750.* New York: W. W. Norton, 1984.

Schermerhorn, Calvin. *Money over Mastery, Family over Freedom: Slavery in the Antebellum Upper South.* Baltimore, MD: Johns Hopkins University Press, 2010.

Schweider, Dorothy, Joseph Hraba, and Elmer Schweider, *Buxton: A Black Utopia in the Heartland.* Iowa City: University of Iowa Press, 2003.

Shaw University, Raleigh. *Twenty-First Annual Catalog of the Officers and Students . . . 1894–1895.* Raleigh, NC: 1895.

Silbey, David J. *A War of Frontier and Empire: The Philippine-American War, 1899–1902.* New York: Hill and Wang, 2007.

Sluiter, Engel. "New Light on the '20. and Odd Negroes' Arriving in Virginia, August 1619." *William and Mary Quarterly* 54 (1997): 395–98.

Smith, James Douglas. "Virginia During Reconstruction, 1865–1870: A Political, Economic and Social Study." PhD diss., University of Virginia, 1960.

Statutes at Large: Being a Collection of the Laws of Virginia, from the First Session of the Legislature, in the year 1619. New York: R. & W. & G. Bartow, 1819–23.

Stek, Pam. "Muchakinock: African Americans and the Making of an Iowa Coal Town." *The Annals of Iowa* 68 (2009): 37–63.

Stevenson, Brenda E. *Life in Black and White: Family and Community in the Slave South.* New York: Oxford University Press, 1996.

Stewart, Richard W., General Editor. *American Military History.* Vol. 1: *The United States Army and the Forging of a Nation, 1775–1917.* Washington, DC: Center of Military History, United States Army, 2005.

Stowell, Daniel W. *Rebuilding Zion: The Religious Reconstruction of the South, 1863–1877.* New York and Oxford: Oxford University Press, 1998.

Thomas, Hugh. *The Slave Trade: The Story of the Atlantic Slave Trade, 1440–1870.* New York: Simon & Schuster, 1997.

Thorndale, William. "The Virginia Census of 1619." *Magazine of Virginia Gene-alogy* 33 (1995): 155–70.

Thornton, John. "The African Experience of the '20. and Odd Negroes' Arriving in Virginia in 1619." *William and Mary Quarterly* 55 (1998): 419–34.

Thorp, Daniel B. "Cohabitation Registers and the Study of Slave Families in Virginia." *Slavery & Abolition* 37 (2016), 744–60.

———. *Facing Freedom: An African American Community in Virginia from Reconstruction to Jim Crow.* Charlottesville: University of Virginia Press, 2017.

———. "Soldiers, Servants, and Very Interested Bystanders: Montgomery County's African American Community During the Civil War." *Virginia Magazine of History and Biography* 126 (2018): 379–421.

Touchstone, Blake. "Planters and Slave Religion in the Deep South." In *Masters and Slaves in the House of the Lord,* edited by John Boles, 99–126. Lexington: University Press of Kentucky, 1988.

Trotter, Joe William, Jr., *Coal, Class, and Color: Blacks in Southern West Virginia, 1915–32.* Urbana: University of Illinois Press, 1990.

Tunc, Tanfer Emin. "The Mistress, the Midwife, and the Medical Doctor: Pregnancy and Childbirth on the Plantations of the Antebellum South, 1800–1860." *Women's History Review* 19 (2010): 395–419.

Von Daacke, Kirt. *Freedom Has a Face: Race, Identity, and Community in Jefferson's Virginia.* Charlottesville: University of Virginia Press, 2012.

Vaughn, Alden T. "Blacks in Virginia: A Note on the First Decade." *William and Mary Quarterly* 29 (1972): 469–78.

Wallace, Lee A., Jr., "The First Regiment of Virginia Volunteers, 1846–1848." *Virginia Magazine of History and Biography* 77 (1969): 46–77.

Walsh, Lorena S. *From Calabar to Carter's Grove: The History of a Virginia Slave Community.* Charlottesville: University Press of Virginia, 1997.

Wedin, Laura Jones. "A Summary of 19th-Century Smithfield, Part 1: The Years Before the Civil War," *Smithfield Review* 18 (2014): 79–96.

———. "A Summary of Nineteenth-Century Smithfield, Part 2: The Early War Years, 1861–1862." *Smithfield Review* 23 (2019): 66–98.

———. "The Preston Cemetery of Historic Smithfield Plantation." *Smithfield Review* 7 (2003): 48–76.

West, Emily. *Family or Freedom: People of Color in the Antebellum South.* Lexington: University of Kentucky Press, 2012.

Whisonant, Robert C. "Geology and History of the Civil War Iron Industry in the New River-Cripple Creek District of Southwestern Virginia." *Virginia Minerals* 44 (November 1998): 25–35.

Whitt, R. Michael. "'Free Indeed!': Trials and Triumphs of Enslaved and Freedmen in Antebellum Virginia," *The Virginia Baptist Register* 50 (2011).

Willis, Wirt H. "The Genesis and Dissolution of William Preston's Smithfield." *Smithfield Review* 8 (2004): 31–38.

Wilson, R. B. "The Dublin Raid." In *G.A.R. War Papers. Papers Read Before Fred. C. Jones Post, No. 401, Department of Ohio, G.A.R.*, edited by E. R. Monfort, H. B. Furness, and Fred. H. Alms, 92–120. Cincinnati, OH: Fred C. Jones Post, No. 401, 1891.

Woods' Baltimore City Directory. Baltimore, MD: John W. Woods, 1883.

Woods' Baltimore City Directory. Baltimore, MD: John W. Woods, 1885.

Woodward, C. Vann, ed. *Mary Chestnut's Civil War.* New Haven, CT: Yale University Press, 1981.

Worsham, Gibson. *Smithfield: Historic Structure Report.* Christiansburg, VA: G. Worsham, 2000.

Wynes, Charles E. *Race Relations in Virginia, 1870–1902.* Charlottesville: University of Virginia Press, 1961.

Zaborney, John J. *Slaves for Hire: Renting Enslaved Laborers in Antebellum Virginia.* Baton Rouge: Louisiana State University Press, 2012.

❖ INDEX ❖

Page references in italics refer to illustrations.

RECENT BOOKS IN
THE AMERICAN SOUTH SERIES